Founded in 1972, the Institute for Research on Public policy is an independent, national, nonprofit organization. Its mission is to improve public policy in Canada by promoting and contributing to a policy process that is more broadly based, informed and effective.

In pursuit of this mission, the IRPP

■ identifies significant public-policy questions that will confront Canada in the longer term future, and undertakes independent research into these questions;

■ promotes wide dissemination of key results from its own and other research activities;

■ encourages non-partisan discussion and criticism of public policy issues by eliciting broad participation from all sectors and regions of Canadian society and linking research with processes of social learning and policy formation.

The IRPP's independence is assured by an endowment fund, to which federal and provincial governments and the private sector have contributed.

iRPP

INSTITUTE FOR RESEARCH ON PUBLIC POLICY

INSTITUT DE RECHERCHE EN POLITIQUES PUBLIQUES

Créé en 1972, l'Institut de recherche en politiques publiques est un organisme national et indépendant à but non lucratif.

L'IRPP a pour mission de favoriser le développement de la pensée politique au Canada par son appui et son apport à un processus élargi, plus éclairé et plus efficace d'élaboration et d'expression des politiques publiques.

Dans le cadre de cette mission, l'IRPP a pour mandat :

■ d'identifier les questions politiques auxquelles le Canada sera confronté dans l'avenir et d'entreprendre des recherches indépendantes à leur sujet;

■ de favoriser une large diffusion des résultats les plus importants de ses propres recherches et de celles des autres sur ces questions;

■ de promouvoir une analyse et une discussion objectives des questions politiques de manière à faire participer activement au débat public tous les secteurs de la société canadienne et toutes les régions du pays, et à rattacher la recherche à l'évolution sociale et à l'élaboration de politiques.

L'indépendance de l'IRPP est assurée par les revenus d'un fonds de dotation auquel ont souscrit les gouvernements fédéral et provinciaux, ainsi que le secteur privé.

INSTITUTE FOR RESEARCH ON PUBLIC POLICY

INSTITUT DE RECHERCHE EN POLITIQUES PUBLIQUES

Workfare;

Does It Work?

Is It Fair?

Patricia M. Evans, Lesley A. Jacobs,

Alain Noël, Elisabeth B. Reynolds

Edited by

Adil Sayeed

Printed in Canada
Bibliothèque nationale du Québec
Dépôt légal 1995

Canadian Cataloguing in Publication Data
Main entry under title:
Workfare : does it work? Is it fair?
(Social policy)
Includes bibliographical references.
ISBN 0-88645-165-5

1. Welfare recipients—Employment—Canada.
2. Public welfare—Canada. 3. Canada-Social policy.
I. Evans, Patricia M. (Patricia Marie), 1944-
II. Sayeed, Adil III. Institute for Research on
Public Policy IV. Series: Social policy (Montréal,Quebec)
HV105.W67 1995   362.5'8,0971   C95-900299-5

Marye Ménard-Bos
Executive Director, IRPP

––––––––––

Monograph Editor
Adil Sayeed

Copy Editor
Mathew Horsman

Design and Production
Schumacher Design

Cover Illustration
Sylvie Deronzier

Published by
The Institute for Research on Public Policy (IRPP)
l'Institut de recherche en politiques publiques
1470 Peel Street, Suite 200
Montreal, Quebec H3A 1T1

Distributed by
Renouf Publishing Co. Ltd.
1294 Algoma Road
Ottawa, Ontario K1B 3W8
For orders, call 613-741-4333
Fax 613-741-5439

––––––––––

Reform is the order of the day for Canada's income security system. However, while almost everyone agrees on the need for change, no consensus has yet emerged on exactly what is required. "Workfare," the notion of linking welfare benefits to participation in public work or training programs, has emerged as a pivotal issue in the debate over income security reform.

Proponents argue that workfare gives recipients the tools to break the trap of long-term welfare dependency and preserves public support for the social safety net. Opponents condemn workfare as a "punish the poor" policy with no real pay off for either welfare beneficiaries or society as a whole.

The debate over workfare crosses traditional ideological dividing lines. Once associated almost exclusively with "conservative" opponents of welfare, in recent years workfare has also been advocated by "moderates" and "liberals" seeking to preserve welfare by reforming it. In the United States, President Bill Clinton has pledged to "end welfare as we know it" by imposing a two-year limit on the receipt of Aid to Families with Dependent Children (AFDC). After two years on AFDC, recipients will be required to take a community service job to maintain their benefits. In Canada, federal Minister of Human Resources Development Lloyd Axworthy raised the workfare issue in his discussion paper, *Improving Social Security in Canada*, by asking Canadians to answer the following question: "Should willingness to participate in employment development services be a condition for the receipt of income support?"

IRPP anticipated the growing interest in workfare in Canada and placed the issue on our social policy research agenda in 1993. We asked Judith Gueron to present an overview of the US experience with welfare-to-work programs at an IRPP Roundtable on Social Policy held in Montreal in June 1993 and published Gueron's paper in our roundtable proceedings, *Income Security in Canada: Changing Needs, Changing Means*.

The roundtable and subsequent discussions with social policy experts confirmed our opinion that workfare remained a critical issue meriting further research. In particular, we concluded that philosophical and political aspects of the issue had been neglected. Research to date has been largely dominated by economic analyses, weighing the costs and benefits of workfare programs for welfare recipients and taxpayers. In assessing the merits of workfare, cost-benefit studies are necessary but not sufficient. We must also consider whether workfare is consistent with our moral values, political traditions and conceptions of social justice.

Accordingly, we commissioned researchers with expertise in different areas to look at various aspects of the workfare issue. In this volume, Lesley Jacobs tests the moral principles put forward to justify workfare; Alain Noël uses a comparative politics model to explain why Canada, the US and Europe adopt different approaches to workfare; Patricia Evans reviews the administration of provincial social assistance programs in Canada and asks whether workfare should be on the provincial policy agenda; and Elisabeth Reynolds presents a case study of a subsidized employment program for social assistance recipients in Quebec. The authors' conclusions should not be attributed to members of IRPP's Board of Directors. However, we are very pleased to publish this collection of informative and thought-provoking papers.

In closing, I would like to thank the dedicated team of professionals responsible for the production of this book. Elisabeth Reynolds helped to develop the concept of a multi-disciplinary review of workfare and to organize an impressive cast of contributors to address different aspects of the issue. IRPP Director of Publications Marye Ménard-Bos has honed supervision of the publication process to a fine art. Chantal Létourneau's meticulous attention to detail was indispensable. As always, Jenny Schumacher and Natalie Coté did a first-class job in designing the publication. Copy Editor Mathew Horsman met his usual standards of excellence and good humour in the face of a tight deadline.

Above all, I am grateful to our four authors. With workfare now at the forefront of the debate over income security reform, this volume is a timely addition to the Institute's series on social policy.

Monique Jérôme-Forget
President, IRPP

CONTENTS

3   FOREWORD

7   INTRODUCTION

13   WHAT ARE THE NORMATIVE FOUNDATIONS
OF WORKFARE?
Lesley A. Jacobs

39   THE POLITICS OF WORKFARE
Alain Noël

75   LINKING WELFARE TO JOBS:
WORKFARE, CANADIAN STYLE
Patricia M. Evans

105   SUBSIDIZED EMPLOYMENT PROGRAMS AND
WELFARE REFORM: THE QUEBEC EXPERIENCE
Elisabeth B. Reynolds

143   NOTES ON CONTRIBUTORS

"**W**orkfare" represents a revival of an old approach to providing state support for the needy. Requiring public work in exchange for public benefits was standard practice as recently as the Great Depression of the 1930s, when help for the unemployed often took the form of "work relief" programs.

However, workfare was not a feature of post-war income security systems. Entitlement to benefits was based on such factors as income, family type, employment status and age, but was generally not conditional on participating in public work, training or other programs aimed at enhancing employability.

In the early 1980s, Charles Murray and other American critics of welfare resurrected the notion of workfare. They argued that compulsory work programs for welfare recipients were necessary to prevent welfare dependency being passed from generation to generation within families. In the United States, preventing long-term dependency has become a dominant concern of welfare policy. As a result, workfare now has broad bipartisan support. In the past year, both President Bill Clinton and the Republican Congressional leadership have proposed legislation that would entrench workfare as a standard feature of the US welfare system.

As workfare has moved up the public policy agenda, the very definition of the concept has evolved. Once narrowly defined as a requirement that employable recipients work or lose all (or at least a portion) of their welfare benefits, a broader conception of workfare now covers all efforts to enhance the employability of welfare recipients. Under the broadest definition, workfare includes both compulsory and voluntary programs aimed at providing welfare recipients with work experience, training and counselling.

To date, Canada has had more experience with voluntary training and employment programs. However, some provinces have introduced an element of compulsion by structuring social assistance to pay lower benefits to employable recipients who do not make themselves available for employment-related programs. And, in its October 1994 discussion paper, *Improving Social Security in Canada*, the federal government raised the option of making Unemployment Insurance (UI) benefits conditional on participation in employment development programs for individuals filing a third UI claim within five years.

The authors of the four studies in this volume confront the workfare issue from four different perspectives. Lesley Jacobs leads off with a discussion of "first principles" underlying workfare. In his chapter, "What Are the Normative Foundations of Workfare?", Jacobs argues that social policies must not only be technically efficient but also consistent with moral values that command broad support within society. He then subjects workfare to this morality test.

Jacobs identifies four normative justifications put forward by advocates of workfare: 1) a work requirement distinguishes the deserving from the undeserving; 2) workfare maintains the self-respect of welfare recipients; 3) the right to income support imposes reciprocal work obligations on recipients; and 4) workfare safeguards welfare recipients' status as citizens able to participate fully in a democratic society. He probes the moral foundations of these four justifications and concludes that only the ideal of "democratic citizenship" stands up as a defensible argument for workfare.

The social status and sense of personal autonomy conveyed by working to support oneself are prerequisites to exercising full rights as a citizen in a democratic society. Ensuring that citizens feel a sense of control over their lives is so critical in a democratic society that compulsory workfare is morally justifiable in some cases, just as education, another fundamental guarantor of democratic citizenship, is compulsory up to a certain age.

Jacobs concludes his chapter by arguing that universal social programs such as public health and education are just as fundamental as work to the sense of common citizenship required to participate in a democratic society. By contrast, targeting of social programs undermines social solidarity and the ideal of democratic citizenship. Ironically, workfare is often paired with targeting measures in proposals to roll back the welfare state. Jacobs' analysis leads him to promote a different policy package. He appeals to the ideal of democratic citizenship to justify workfare within a broader system of universal social programs.

Alain Noël then looks at how social values affect the political culture and policy approaches of different countries. In "The Politics of Workfare," he explores the thesis that a country's approach to workfare will reflect the political traditions underlying its welfare state model. For example, the US is a bastion of economic liberalism. In that country, the standard presumption has been that welfare recipients lack a strong enough work ethic to avail themselves of the job opportunities generated by the free market. Thus, American workfare is aimed at deterring recipients from becoming dependent on welfare. Because liberal political cultures also seek to minimize government expenditure, workfare is promoted as a way to cut welfare spending. Unfortunately, effective work, training and counselling programs entail upfront costs. If the long-run savings from reduced welfare dependency do not exceed the costs of workfare programs, then a liberal welfare state such as the US faces a dilemma. Requiring welfare recipients to work is popular, but paying for workfare is not.

Noël believes that conservative welfare states such as Germany and France share the US' concern with restraining government spending. However, the conservative approach to workfare differs from that of the liberal US in one important respect. In Germany and France, there is a stronger tendency to attribute joblessness and welfare to problems in the way the labour market works, rather than to an inadequate work ethic among welfare recipients. According to this view, the welfare problem stems from a mismatch between the skills required for available jobs and the skills of the unemployed. The solution is to provide "active" programs such as training and work experience to raise the skill levels of the unemployed and increase their chances of employment.

In other words, Germany and France use work and training programs to give welfare recipients a hand, while the US gives recipients a push. Despite this difference, conservative and liberal states face a similar dilemma. Their interest in workfare is circumscribed by their interest in controlling government expenditures.

Social democratic states such as Sweden share the conservative diagnosis that a mismatch in the labour market is the source of the welfare problem. However, social democrats are more willing to fund programs to raise recipients' skill levels. The social democratic dilemma stems from a concern that work and training programs aimed at the unemployed and welfare recipients are paternalistic and not consistent with the values of social solidarity and universality underlying the social democratic welfare state.

Noël then applies his model to Canada, which he views as a "hybrid" welfare state — predominantly liberal in its use of means-testing of income transfers, but with some social democratic elements such as universal public health care and some conservative features such as more generous benefits for families than for single people. Thus, Noël concludes that, while Canada may well adopt the US model of compulsory workfare aimed at deterring people from going on and staying on welfare, there is a chance for a more comprehensive and skills-oriented set of European-style work and training programs to emerge.

Jacobs and Noël provide guides to the philosophy and politics of workfare. Patricia Evans follows with a review of workfare in practice. In her chapter, "Linking Welfare to Jobs: Workfare, Canadian Style," Evans reports on recent developments at the provincial level in Canada. She stresses that social assistance has never been completely unconditional for employable recipients, who have to show that they are available and willing to work. Requirements that recipients show proof of job search activity have been and are being enforced with varying degrees of rigour in different provinces at different times.

Evans identifies three provincial approaches indicative of a growing trend toward workfare in Canada. First, some provinces have moved to categorize employable social assistance recipients according to their willingness to participate in work-related programs. Those categorized as non-participants receive lower benefits than participants. Second, provinces are directing more voluntary work experience and employment subsidy programs at social assistance recipients. Third, some provinces are encouraging recipients to commit themselves to "action plans" or "contracts" outlining a program of training, job search and other activities designed to enhance employability.

In addition, provinces are experimenting with improving the incentives for social assistance recipients to return to the work force. Such measures include lowering the rates at which social assistance benefits are reduced as earnings increase, earnings supplements for low-income families with children and proposals to replace the child portion of social assistance benefits with an income-tested child tax credit. Voluntary training programs aimed at upgrading the skills and employability of social assistance recipients represent another approach. Evans argues that these types of "carrots" are more likely to be successful at reducing welfare dependency than workfare "sticks."

Evans concludes her chapter with a comparison of the US and Swedish approaches. She prefers the Swedish commitment to providing the unemployed with public works jobs and training to the American penchant for punishing welfare recipients for not working. Thus, she recommends that Canada follow Sweden's model of active support for the unemployed, rather than the US model of punitive, compulsory workfare.

Evans' comprehensive overview of recent developments at the provincial level is followed by a case study of Quebec program to assist social assistance recipients to move back into the work force. In her chapter, "Subsidized Employment Programs and Welfare Reform: The Quebec Experience," Elisabeth Reynolds presents some preliminary results on the *Programme d'aide à l'intégration en emploi* (PAIE).

Quebec's 1987 welfare reforms divided social assistance cases into two broad categories, employable and non-employable. Employable cases receive the *Actions positives pour le travail et l'emploi* (APTE) benefit. APTE recipients are, in turn, divided into four categories: those participating in employment-related programs, those available to participate once a program space becomes available, those temporarily unavailable due to circumstances (e.g., child care responsibilities) and those who choose not to participate. APTE benefits are structured such that participants receive the most, while non-participants receive the least.

PAIE, one of the employment-related programs for APTE recipients, was introduced in May 1990. It subsidizes wages for up to six months for APTE recipients placed with either private or public sector employers. Following the completion of their subsidized work experience, PAIE participants were tracked over a period of 19 months. Their employment and welfare experience was compared with a similar group of APTE recipients who did not participate in PAIE or any other employment-related program but who shared characteristics with participants in terms of age, sex and education.

Results show that, relative to the comparison group, a higher percentage of PAIE participants were employed at least once during the 19-month follow-up period. Furthermore, PAIE participants were employed for longer periods than comparison group members and a higher percentage of PAIE participants stayed off welfare after finding a job.

These preliminary PAIE results are consistent with previous studies showing that the benefits of US programs providing employment subsidies for welfare recipients outweighed costs. However, Reynolds cautions that it is too early to reach a definitive conclusion about the cost-effectiveness of PAIE.

Thus, each author looks at workfare from a different angle: Jacobs probes the moral foundations of workfare; Noël shows how differences in social values across countries lead to different approaches to workfare; Evans presents a progress report on workfare trends in Canada; and Reynolds focusses on one Quebec program aimed at enhancing employment prospects of social assistance recipients. We hope that this collection of studies will serve as a starting point for an informed public debate on this important issue.

Adil Sayeed
Research Director, Social Policy
IRPP

L E S L E Y   A .   J A C O B S

What Are the Normative

Foundations of Workfare?

Introduction

Traditionally, in Canada, social welfare programs have operated through the use of cash and in-kind redistributive transfers whereby beneficiaries of these programs have received either income supplements in the form of cash or access to specific goods and services such as health care and subsidized housing. The main debates over principle have revolved around whether these programs should be directed universally at all Canadians or targeted to specific disadvantaged groups within Canadian society. The recent effort by the federal government as well as a number of provincial governments to introduce new "workfare-style" programs into the Canadian social safety net is widely regarded as an attempt to shift debates over principles to a different arena.[1] Redistributive transfers, whether in-kind or cash, are a payment by the government to an individual that does not arise out of current productive activity. Workfare measures, in contrast, make such payments conditional on the individual performing some sort of work or participating in a job training scheme. Workfare is commonly thought to reflect a new public philosophy of social policy, one that differs radically from the public philosophy that has dominated the building of the welfare state in Canada over the past 40 years. The important point is that the embrace of workfare is regarded as not just a stance on a particular social policy, but also as a rejection of the dominant public ethos on social welfare in Canada in favour of a bold, new way of thinking about the country's welfare state.

This context suggests that an adequate analysis of workfare must attend to both practical, technical questions about how a workfare program might be designed and implemented in a Canadian setting *and* normative questions about what sort of moral values and principles underlie the very idea of workfare. Although I provide, as a preliminary exercise, a rough sketch of what a Canadian-style workfare program might look like, this chapter is designed mainly to address the second class of questions. Despite the obvious importance of these normative questions, there has not been any careful and systematic attempt to address them within a Canadian context. My purpose in this chapter is to provide an accessible review and evaluation of the possible normative foundations of workfare. Among defenders of the concept, there is little consensus around the moral principles that underlie this sort of social policy. Instead, various proponents of workfare appeal to very different moral values in their attempts to ground their views. (This fact, combined with loose use of the term, "workfare," explains in my view why defenders of the concept tend to cut across the political spectrum.) I focus below on the four most common and influential normative arguments for workfare. Ultimately, I argue that the most promising defence is one that appeals to an ideal of democratic citizenship embedded in Canadian political culture. This defence implies, however, that rather than replace the extensive network of universal social programs that exists at present in Canada, workfare programs should complement many of those existing, more fundamental programs.

SOME BACKGROUND ON WORKFARE

Before addressing in depth the various normative arguments in favour of workfare, it may be helpful to expand on my introductory remarks in two ways. First, I shall say a bit more about the general approach to public policy taken in this chapter. Second, I shall sketch out a sample Canadian-style workfare program so that it will be clearer what exactly I mean in this chapter by workfare.

Values and Public Policy

So far, I have assumed that moral values and normative justifications for public policy matter when we think about reforming Canada's welfare state institutions. For some people, this assumption may seem surprising. Many analyses of public policy contain little reference to moral values and questions of social justice. Typically, economists and public administrators rigorously separate disputes over the *aims* or ends of a policy and disagreements over the *means* or methods to be used for achieving those aims or ends.[2] For any social policy, we, first, want to know its aims and, then, how best to achieve them. The aims involve normative judgements about moral values and principles — in particular, issues of social justice. Aims tend to be controversial and widely, if not essentially, contested. They fall within the domain of moral and political philosophy. For instance, the aim of an income tax policy might be a fair distribution of income among citizens; what is fair is obviously a normative judgement. Separate from questions about aims are questions about means. If you assume that the aim is settled, what then is the best means of achieving it? This is ordinarily treated as a technical question that can be addressed by economists and social policy analysts. For example, assuming a specific standard of fairness is in place, it is a technical question to ask what rate of progressive taxation will achieve a fair distribution of income.

In my view, this attempt to separate rigorously the aims and the means of social policy is frequently a mistake. I believe, on the contrary, the following: sometimes the aim — the justification for a social policy — entails the particular measure or means that should be used to achieve it.[3] My point is that, often, choosing the means is not merely a technical matter; it requires careful consideration of the moral values and normative arguments that underlie the policy choice. This means that economists and public policy analysts cannot treat disputes over the instruments of social policy as purely technical matters; they must take seriously philosophical debates about the nature of social justice in order to determine which social program should be implemented.

My broader point is that it is difficult to see how in Canada we can seriously try to reform our existing scheme of social programs without also examining in some depth the principles of social justice that underlie them. Presumably, those principles of social justice will dictate to a significant degree the possible paths for reform.

This is directly relevant to my discussion of the normative foundations of workfare. Defenders of workfare generally seek to argue not only that in some instances it is preferable to existing social programs on technical grounds but also that it dovetails better with certain powerful moral values and principles of social justice that are widely held in Canada. Conversely, critics of workfare typically argue not only that there are technical problems but also that it runs contrary to the aims of Canadian social policy. By clarifying and evaluating the possible normative grounds for workfare, this chapter is designed to make a distinctive contribution to the emerging debate over workfare in Canada.

A Workfare Program for Canada

What exactly is workfare? How would a workfare program operate? How would it fit into the existing social safety net in Canada? What would it replace? I shall briefly address these important questions here. My comments are intended to bring more clearly into focus the type of social program that drives the justificatory arguments for workfare we shall examine later in the chapter.

Although serious discussion of workfare is a recent phenomenon in Canada, the idea has received careful attention in the United States for nearly a decade. Initially, it was closely associated with conservative social policy analysts such as Charles Murray and Lawrence Mead.[4] However, by the late 1980s, some people claimed that in Washington there was a new consensus across the political spectrum around the introduction of workfare into American social policy.[5] Evidence of this consensus is the support for certain (in some cases quite restricted) workfare measures by such noted liberal social policy analysts as David Ellwood, Christopher Jencks and Mickey Kaus.[6] Much of the American discussion has focussed on the question of how to introduce workfare-style measures into particular social programs, especially Aid for Families with Dependent Children (AFDC). The most important piece of legislation has been the 1988 Family Support Act. For Canadians, however, these American debates about how to implement workfare are not particularly instructive since we have a very different set of redistributive social programs.

It is worth noting, nonetheless, one area where American research does seem relevant in the Canadian context. Many advocates of workfare are concerned about the effect of Canadian social programs on the motivation of the unemployed to get a job. They worry that existing social welfare undermines the incentive to work, and thereby threatens the work ethic that is central to our economy. Exhaustive American studies suggest that there is little social scientific basis for this worry. As for the beneficial effects of workfare on incentives, most American studies have been inconclusive.[7] The upshot is important because it means that a successful defence of workfare must appeal to something other than claims about incentives.

For the most part, proponents of workfare in Canada have focussed on reforming either unemployment insurance (UI) or social assistance (welfare) or both. For the sake of brevity, I shall outline here only a proposal to reform welfare. In 1993, nearly three million people in Canada collected welfare. This represented 10.4 percent of the population. Welfare payments by provincial governments and municipalities totalled $14.3 billion. According to the National Council of Welfare, in 1992 among households that collected welfare the head of the household was employable in 45 percent of the cases.[8] Workfare measures would focus on those households where the head of the household is employable but not working. In effect, a workfare program would make the receipt of welfare benefits conditional on participation by that head of household in either a public works project or some sort of job training scheme. Some sort of child care program for single-parent households would have to exist in parallel to any such workfare program.

Let me elaborate on the details of such a program by responding to two important criticisms that are often made of workfare. The first is that workfare necessarily involves low-skilled, poorly paid work with few long-term prospects. Certainly, it is the case that many proposals have indeed involved work of this calibre, especially in the US. For example, Mickey Kaus in his influential book, *The End of Equality*, outlines a workfare scheme where the government would set up job sites and practically all of the labour would be manual — e.g., cleaning, painting, filling potholes *etc*.[9] Recent workfare-style proposals by the Chrétien government have also been accused of having this character.[10] However, I would like to stress that workfare does not necessarily have to involve work that lacks intrinsic value and requires few skills. The Works Projects Administration (WPA) is an historical example that illustrates my point that workfare can involve useful, dignified, high-skill and meaningful jobs.[11] WPA was an important part of President Franklin

Roosevelt's 1935 New Deal scheme for addressing high unemployment in the US. Basically, it was a program where the government provided work on a wide range of projects to more than three million people. Roosevelt's vision of WPA emphasized work that was socially useful, as opposed to so-called "make-work" projects. Most people associate WPA with the building of infrastructure projects such as highways, bridges, airports, parks *etc.* However, an important component of the WPA were the projects designed specifically for artists and writers. These included, for example, a project for writers to produce travel guides to various regions of the US, guides which are unique and still have a significant readership among tourists. What I am suggesting is that workfare does not necessarily mean uninteresting or insignificant work.

Let us then turn to the second important criticism. Most defenders of workfare focus initially on the claim that, generally, work is preferable to welfare. This claim has, at least in our society, a certain commonsensical power to it. After all, most of us would prefer that our government be concerned with job creation than with remedial programs such as welfare measures that address existing unemployment. Most critics of workfare agree with this point. The controversial feature of workfare is, therefore, not the idea that work is preferable to welfare but rather the non-voluntary dimension of workfare. Workfare makes the receipt of benefits conditional on participation in one of the government's job or training schemes. It compels people to participate. Sometimes, this non-voluntary feature of workfare is defended on the grounds of incentives; if participation was voluntary, then people would not have the motivation to participate. However, if you concede, as I have above, that the social scientific literature on the links among welfare, workfare and incentives is inconclusive, then it becomes much trickier to justify the non-voluntary feature of workfare.[12] How else can this feature be justified? My answer is derived from the observation that non-voluntary participation in social programs is a standard feature of Canada's welfare state. The best examples are the Canada Pension Plan and provincial health care schemes. We are compelled to contribute to these programs. The standard justification for this compulsion is not, however, an incentive argument. Ordinarily, the non-voluntary dimension is justified on the grounds that either it is necessary to collectivize risk or because it is a form of "binded rationality," that is to say, the state binds us to participate in order to protect us from a myopic tendency. Presumably, either of these two grounds could justify the non-voluntary feature of workfare.

By way of a final comment, it should be obvious that in my view implementing workfare will not be, at least in the short-run, a money-saving program for government. The principal reason is that the costs of implementing a well-designed workfare scheme will be much higher than the initial savings from reduced welfare payments. For public officials, it is essential to decide whether their commitment, in the course of reforming social programs, is to saving money or to improving the social safety net for Canadians by better facilitating the welfare-to-work transition. Evidence from the US suggests well-run workfare programs will not serve both of these objectives.[13]

FOUR NORMATIVE ARGUMENTS FOR WORKFARE

I now turn to a critical examination of four possible and, one hopes, familiar normative arguments advanced in favour of workfare. I assume that the objective of each of these arguments is to defend the implementation of something like the Canadian-style workfare program I have just outlined. It is also important to keep in mind that often these four arguments are not carefully distinguished; instead, the claims of some arguments are conflated with those of others. From the point of view of critically evaluating them, this task of clearly distinguishing each argument is fundamental.

The Argument from Desert

Few ideas about the theory of the welfare state have proven to be more controversial than the notion of a "deserving" poor. The main idea that has driven such a notion is that sound social policy should allow us to distinguish among the poor and disadvantaged those who deserve help from the government and those who do not. Among social policy makers and political elites, this notion has been harshly received over the past 30 years. Defenders of the modern welfare state, especially in Canada and Western Europe, have regarded such a notion as reminiscent of an earlier, less progressive stage in redistributive social policy, one that we associate with Victorian Poor Law. Despite this hostile reception, the idea of a deserving poor appears still to have a strong residual appeal among the general public.[14] Some have sought to defend workfare over redistributive transfers on the grounds that as a social policy measure it identifies and helps only the "deserving" poor. This defence gives work-fare a populist flavour.

This argument from desert for workfare involves two especially important elements. The first element revolves around the question of who exactly are the "deserving" poor. The deserving poor, according to this argument, are those who are willing to work but, because of bad luck, do not have the opportunity to do so. The supposed contrast is to those who are poor and disadvantaged because they are lazy and irresponsible. The second element has to do with what sort of social policy might track this standard of desert. Typically, the redistributive transfers that prevail in Canada's social safety net are said not to be sensitive to this standard of desert. Workfare, in contrast, is defended because it tracks desert, so understood. Workfare schemes are said to reward only those willing to work. It denies benefits to those who lazy and indolent.

I shall argue that this defence of workfare based on desert presupposes an overly simplistic notion of desert and that any attempt to ground workfare on a more complex standard is bound to fail.

Among modern moral and political philosophers, there is little agreement about the concept of desert. Some think that it is at the very core of justice.[15] They question how it is possible to even conceive of justice without a prior understanding of the concept of desert. At the other extreme, some utilitarian philosophers believe the concept has no real role in a theory of morality.[16] For them, desert is an empty notion without the sort of critical potential we associate with the concept of justice. Others accept that while the concept may be important, it is such a vague and imprecise standard that we are ill advised to give it a foundational role in our notions of social justice. Perhaps the most famous statement of this view is John Rawls' book, *A Theory of Justice*, where standards of desert are not assumed to have a prior and independent place in a theory of justice but instead are treated as a function of more basic principles of liberty and equality.[17] For Rawls, justice requires respect of individuals as free and equal people; what they can be said to deserve flows from our understanding of this requirement. Still, others give desert a primary place but insist that it is but one among a series of competing values, including equality.[18] Their view is that justice requires us to strike a balance among these various values. We cannot here expand in any depth on this controversy within philosophical circles. However, drawing attention to this debate is significant because it suggests that we should have serious reservations about social policy reform predicated on a view of desert as an unproblematic concept.

Perhaps even more to the point is the criticism that, when notions of desert prevail in debates about public policy, the actual standard applied is one that reflects the dominant social group.[19] The force of this critique is evident in the context of examining systemic discrimination experienced by women in the workplace.[20] It is well known that in Canada there is a division of labour within the family and that women carry out a disproportionate share of the domestic labour. This is especially the case when it comes to child care. The issue of systemic discrimination in the workplace arises when these injustices within the family affect women's opportunities in the workplace. Often, certain opportunities in the labour market are structured in ways that, although they do not overtly discriminate against women in the sense that there are legal barriers denying women access, make it impossible for women carrying a significant burden of domestic labour to compete for those opportunities. Typically, when women are unsuccessful at securing such opportunities because of demands made on them by the division of labour within the family, this is justified on the grounds of some sort of notion of desert — the men who secured the opportunities "deserved" them more. But clearly this sort of argument reflects a standard of desert which inherently is stacked against most women in Canada; it favours men. The dominance of such a standard constitutes a form of gender disadvantage in the workplace. An important upshot of this analysis of gender disadvantage in the workplace is that, from the perspective of social justice, we need a more dynamic standard of desert that is sensitive to differences between people.

This is relevant to the workfare debate insofar as we should be sceptical of any appeal to a standard of desert that is very narrow. In fact, most proponents of the argument from desert acknowledge this point. Few defend, for instance, applying a work requirement to the elderly or those who suffer severe physical or mental disabilities. Likewise, no one seriously defends workfare for children. (In Canada in 1993, 37 percent of the recipients of welfare were children.) But even for those who are "employable," the issue is a good deal more complex. Some of the strongest proponents of workfare admit, for example, that a distinctive disadvantage suffered by the poor and long-term unemployed is a lack of confidence, not of a willingness to work *per se*.[21] This means, then, that applying a certain standard of desert that emphasizes only willingness to work seems unfair. Other observations further complicate the point. Few people seriously challenge the claim that family background significantly influences life chances. This is disturbing because, as numerous political philosophers have emphasized, the family you are born into is a matter of luck; a child does not "deserve" to be born into a particular family. Family background, then, is morally arbitrary.[22] More controversial is the effort to extend this reasoning from family background to the possession of natural endowments. The main idea here is that what natural endowments you have is a matter of genetic luck; like your socioeconomic background, those endowments cannot be said to be something you "deserve." The distribution of natural endowments is, from a moral point of view, arbitrary.[23] The challenge, then, is to formulate a concept of desert that accommodates all of these complexities.

This is not just an intellectual challenge. For those who advance the view that the normative foundations of workfare rest on the notion of desert, it is necessary for them to explain why workfare is a better way to track desert than welfare, which uses traditional redistributive transfers. Is workfare a better instrument for identifying those who are "deserving?" That claim may seem plausible if you assume an overly simplistic notion of desert. However, if the complexities just mentioned are taken seriously, it seems much less plausible. It seems hard to imagine that a workfare program could be designed that would accommodate all of the differences among those who might be said to be "deserving." If we did want to design a single social program that tracks desert in all its complexities, it seems much more plausible to implement some sort of guaranteed basic income that allows for desert-based inequalities above the social minimum.[24]

The Argument from Self-Respect

I have just shown that the argument from desert is incapable of providing normative foundations for workfare. Here, I examine critically the argument that workfare is preferable to welfare because it better promotes the self-respect of the individuals who benefit from these sorts of government programs.[25]

This argument relies on a particularly powerful critique of the reliance on redistributive cash and in-kind transfers that prevails in existing social policy. This critique can be briefly summarized:

1. Redistributive transfers are designed to meet an individual's needs.

2. Among any individual's needs is having self-respect where self-respect is understood as "one's belief that one lives up to certain [socially determined] standards that define what it is to be a person of worth, a person entitled to respect."[26]

3. In our society, the most important socially determined standard for measuring one's self-respect is the idea that one works for what one receives.

4. Redistributive transfers involve payments that have not arisen out of current productive activity.

5. Therefore, redistributive transfers have a self-defeating aspect in that they frustrate some of the needs of the recipient in the course of meeting other needs he or she has.

It is not my intention to challenge the cogency of this critique of redistributive transfers. I believe it successfully pinpoints a genuine problem with conventional social policy. The inference I am concerned to challenge, however, is the further claim that workfare is therefore a better way to meet the needs of individuals.

This normative defence rests on the argument that, unlike redistributive transfers, workfare does not threaten the recipient's self-respect and therefore cannot be said to have a self-defeating aspect to it. This argument appears plausible, I think, because under a workfare scheme the unemployed and disadvantaged are given the opportunity to meet their own needs by working for what they receive. But notice that this defence of workfare depends on the further inference that the use of workfare does not threaten the self-respect of the unemployed and disadvantaged. There is, however, an elementary problem with this inference.

Suppose that an individual is given a job because he or she is part of a workfare scheme and not because he or she "earned" it. What I question is whether anyone who is given a job in this fashion will not experience some degree of threat to their self-respect. The puzzle is how exercising the opportunity to work provided by a workfare scheme would not have the effect of undermining an individual's self-respect, thus introducing a self-defeating aspect into the use of workfare as a way to meet needs.[27] After all, if you have to take up a job offer from a government workfare program, it is hard to see how, from the perspective of self-respect, this would be any different from accepting a redistributive transfer.

Now, someone might respond that, although it is true that the use of workfare does have a self-defeating aspect, it is still preferable to the use of redistributive transfers because it undermines the self-respect of the recipient less than does the use of transfers. The validity of this response depends, I think, on just how much redistributive transfers do in fact undermine the self-respect of the recipient. I shall make two remarks which combined are intended to show that, contrary to what some proponents of workfare claim, the negative effects of redistributive transfers on self-respect are unlikely to be significantly different from those arising from workfare measures.

First of all, notice that the argument I sketched out above does not actually establish that all redistributive transfers designed to meet needs pose a threat to self-respect. There are two possible ways in which a transfer to someone might be redistributive. It might be either redistributive *between* different people or redistributive *across* one person's life. A social program providing everyone with the same benefits is an example of a program redistributive between people if it is funded through a progressive income tax with the effect that high earners are subsidizing the benefits received by low earners. A mandatory contribution scheme for old-age pensions is an example of a program that is primarily intended to be redistributive across one person's lifetime. The idea is that you contribute when you are young and working so that you have an income when you are older and no longer working. (This is still an example of a redistributive transfer because the payment of the pension does not arise out of current productive activity.) Redistribution in this second sense — across one person's life — was the primary objective in the setting up of the British and Canadian welfare state after the Second World War. It is hard to see how the use of transfer payments that are redistributive across one person's life would threaten the recipient's self-respect. This is significant since, in Canada, many social programs have this character.

My second and more important remark concerns the empirical claim that the degree to which a redistributive transfer threatens a recipient's self-respect is a function of whether society regards that transfer as an act of charity or as the fulfilment of a right required by social justice. The received view is that a rights-based redistributive transfer regarded as a requirement of social justice will threaten the recipient's self-respect less than a transfer regarded as charity.[28] It follows that provided the social safety net in Canada is regarded as just, the use of transfers will not have a more harmful effect on the self-respect of the recipient than workfare measures. The point for a Canadian government sincerely committed to just social policy is that it is very important for the government to maintain public support for welfare state measures. It is well known that the existence of universally accessible programs in areas such as health care, pensions, child allowance and education play an extremely important role in maintaining this support.[29] Governments that reduce the level of accessibility of such programs inadvertently undermine public support for the welfare state.

The Argument from Social Responsibility

So far, I have argued that, on normative grounds, workfare cannot be defended on the basis that it tracks desert or that it better promotes self-respect. I turn here to the argument that the normative foundations of workfare rest on the potential of workfare programs to promote social responsibility. This argument has been influential in the US and, I suspect, has significant appeal in Canada.

The background context for this argument is a public arena where the language of rights is perceived to be on the increase and, indeed, is so pervasive that practically all political issues are expressed as either the violation of rights or the fulfilment of rights. The dominance of rights discourse in Canada is widely associated with the implementation of the Charter of Rights and Freedoms as part of the 1982 constitutional package. Our thinking about social policy has not escaped this rights discourse. The idea of welfare rights has, however, been central to the progressive reforms to the welfare state in Canada since the Second World War. Addressing questions of socio-economic disadvantage is now predominantly presented as a matter of rights. This reflects, as I mentioned above, the transition from regarding social policy as an instance of government charity to an issue of justice. Typically, Canada is believed to be following the lead of the US, where the language of rights and entitlements is seen to dominate the political landscape.

This dominance of rights discourse has not, however, gone unchallenged. Certain critics of the Canadian Charter of Rights and Freedoms have argued that the legalization of issues of social justice constitutes a threat to our democratic institutions and have urged a retreat from our obsession with rights.[30] In the US, a central theme of a range of writings on the issue of individual rights has been that the dominance of rights discourse has had a devastating impact on public institutions. The practice of rights supposedly engenders a deeply rooted individualism which threatens the sense of community and shared commitment that is foundational to American public life.[31] Citizenship is said to involve not only rights, but also to entail fundamental duties.

Advocates have seized on this argument to defend workfare.[32] The problem, it is said, with viewing welfare benefits as an issue of rights or entitlements is that this has led to a neglect of the social responsibility of the welfare recipient. In a scheme involving redistributive transfers, individuals stand on their rights and demand benefits. They focus, in other words, on what they are owed. But this neglects what they owe their political community in return. The implicit idea is that a scheme of social welfare presupposes a measure of reciprocity; people are required to make contributions to the scheme, not just withdrawals. Making the practice of welfare rights and entitlements central to a scheme of social welfare distorts this idea of reciprocity. The case for workfare rests on the claim that workfare programs are designed to correct this imbalance between rights and duties. The main idea is that the work requirement for the collection of welfare benefits is a mere reflection of what the recipient owes to his or her community, as a matter of duty. Workfare, unlike the existing social assistance programs, imposes on people social responsibility. And the importance of social responsibility has been overlooked in our social policy because of our ill-conceived obsession with rights.

Much of the power of the argument from social responsibility in favour of workfare derives from the background claim that rights and duties are closely linked. Now, I do not intend to dispute that background claim,[33] nor, indeed, the proposition that social policy, like other realms of public policy, should be more sensitive to social responsibility. However, it seems to me that there is a relatively simple, but nonetheless *decisive*, problem with this argument from social responsibility.[34] The problem is that, while defenders of workfare who rely on the argument from social responsibility may be right to say that social policy should be concerned with promoting social responsibility among welfare recipients, they fail to show that workfare is a better way to do this than other social programs such as, for example, a scheme that enables individuals from a wide range of socio-economic backgrounds to work on community projects organized by volunteer and charitable societies.

Let me explain. Proponents of the argument from social responsibility typically emphasize that long-term recipients of welfare not only do not work, but more specifically behave differently from mainstream Canadians and Americans because they have not internalized the commitment to work and to making a contribution to society. Existing social policy supposedly promotes this form of "dependency" and a parasitic approach to others in their political community. These defenders of workfare lament for a time when everyone accepted his or her social responsibilities and shouldered a share of the burden. The question I am pressing is why they think we should introduce workfare to promote this sense of social responsibility, rather than some other social program.

The force of this question can be illustrated by reference to Britain. There, it is widely believed that over the past 15 years there has been a significant decline in people's acceptance of this sense of social responsibility. (It is standardly blamed in particular on the policies and practices of the Thatcher government.) However, the most cogent policy responses have not involved an appeal to workfare. For example, in May 1994, the Commission on Social Justice proposed what it called a Citizens' Service. The principal objective of such a service is "the renewal of this country's civic life."[35] The main idea is that young adults from all different socioeconomic backgrounds be given the opportunity to join a program for an average of three months, participating in volunteer service activities in return for a small stipend and some sort of educational or UI credit. The point would be to promote the social responsibilities of citizenship by educating young people about and involving them in the public sphere of their political community. From the point of view of promoting social responsibility, this sort of program is superior to workfare because it is directed at everyone, not just the poor and disadvantaged. After all, if you take seriously the claim that the dominance of rights discourse has led to the decline in social responsibility, then this decline must also be prevalent among people other than the poor and disadvantaged.[36] Hence, programs designed to promote social responsibility should be directed at all citizens.

My objection, then, to the argument from social responsibility is that while it may be right to say that we should have social programs that promote a sense of social responsibility and the idea that rights and entitlements entail duties, it is doubtful that this warrants the introduction of workfare. At a minimum, a careful analysis of proposals such as the Citizens' Service in the UK is necessary to show why we should introduce workfare instead of these alternative programs.

The Argument from Democratic Citizenship

I turn now to what I regard as the most plausible normative argument for workfare. At the centre of this argument is a particular ideal of democratic citizenship. It is generally beyond dispute that in Canada we aspire to be a democracy. We strive to be a political community where certain important decisions are made collectively and we govern ourselves. Although the exact details of this democratic vision of politics remain controversial, as do the structure of the corresponding social and political institutions, our attraction to democracy is driven partially by the ideal of individual citizens living together and having a significant amount of control over their lives.[37] The point is that democratic institutions offer to us the possibility of being to some degree self-governing. As opposed to other forms of governments where citizens are merely the passive subjects of legislation and public policy, democratic government promotes and, in fact, relies on a social practice of active citizenship where individual citizens are not just subject to the law but, to a certain degree, actually generate it.

What are the implications of this ideal of active democratic citizenship for social policy? In my view, the implications are significant in so far as how social policy should be *delivered* in Canada. Many existing social welfare programs do not live up to this idea of active citizenship and, indeed, often seem designed to subvert it. Combined with a "come and get it" design which has built-in biases against certain citizens,[38] these programs treat people as the passive recipients of benefits that discourage them from taking control of their own lives. The recent preoccupation with "welfare dependency" is, from the perspective of democratic citizenship, worrisome not because certain individuals constitute potentially an endless drain on public resources but rather because dependency runs counter to the ideal of citizens actively controlling their own lives.

Before explaining the link between workfare and democratic citizenship, let me just briefly distinguish my claim that the ideal of democratic citizenship has significant implications for how social programs should be delivered from the very different claim that our shared democratic citizenship grounds why we should have redistributive social programs in the first place. This second claim addresses the following question: why should the government redistribute income and other resources from some citizens to other citizens? Some people think that the answer lies in our shared citizenship in a democratic society.[39] My own view is that an appeal to shared citizenship to justify redistributive social policy evades the attacks on redistribution from conservatives, rather than addresses them.[40] As Charles Murray puts it in his influential book, *Losing Ground*, "Why should one person give *anything* to a stranger whose only claim to his help is a common citizenship?"[41] In response to challenges by conservatives such as Murray, I have argued at length elsewhere that rights to basic liberties can provide the normative basis for redistributive welfare state measures such as those that exist in Canada.[42] My claim is, in effect, that these sorts of measures meet certain needs that are necessary for anyone to be the sort of person who can be said to enjoy rights to basic liberties.

Democratic societies are, as I said above, driven by this vision of citizens with some control over their lives. In our society, work is the most effective way to realize this control. Having employment earnings is obviously an important reason why work is such an effective way to have some control over one's life. But being unemployed is not just a matter of not having employment earnings. There are benefits other than income that go with having a job, most obviously the development and enhancement of job skills: you have better job opportunities when you are employed, simply because you already have a job. Other long-term benefits, such as pension contributions, are not addressed in current welfare or unemployment legislation. It is also well established that those who suffer from long-term unemployment suffer much more from ill-health, depression and low self-esteem.

An example illustrates the point. Much of the effort in the disability-rights movement in Canada has recently been directed at making educational institutions more accessible to the disabled, and at challenging barriers that prevent those with disabilities from pursuing certain employment prospects. Implicit in this initiative is the astute observation that work provides the best means for disabled Canadians to realize control over their own lives. This reflects a significant shift in social policy from providing the disabled with cash redistributive transfers to emphasizing work and training opportunities. Workfare, too, is radical precisely because it proposes to treat the unemployed and disadvantaged as active citizens who should not be made dependent on others but instead should be encouraged and empowered to take control of their own lives by having work and job training opportunities.

The main point is that workfare is attractive for democratic citizenship because it is focussed on providing people with work so that they can take control of their own lives instead of being dependent on others. From this perspective, workfare is a progressive social policy because it enables the poor and disadvantaged to become active democratic citizens. (This is not to deny that exercising opportunities to work provided by a workfare program may undermine to some degree an individual's self-respect.) Unlike the argument from social responsibility, the emphasis is on what workfare does for each individual citizen, as opposed to what it does for the civic life of the political community. The focus is on workfare as a program for fulfilling the right to work of all citizens in a democratic society, rather than on the duties of welfare recipients to contribute to the well-being of their community.

Notice that I have just now suggested that workfare can be grounded on the idea that citizens in a democracy have a right to work. The principal reason why I think that the ascription of a right to work to each citizen makes sense in a democracy is that such a right would seem to flow logically from the ideal of active democratic citizenship outlined above.[43] After all, if democratic citizenship requires that individuals have significant control over their lives and work is a basic ingredient for that control, then it seems reasonable to ascribe to citizens a right to work.[44]

Now, this shift, in the context of a discussion of workfare, to the language of a right to work may be surprising. One reason is that frequently workfare is regarded as a social policy antagonistic to the rights of welfare recipients. (This is, of course, a central theme in arguments about social responsibility and desert, discussed above.) In particular, the fact that workfare compels those drawing benefits to work, rather than making it voluntary, has struck many as contrary to the very notion of a right to work. But it seems clear that this objection rests on a conceptual mistake about the nature of rights. There is nothing problematic about saying someone has a right to something and compelling them to exercise that right. Perhaps the clearest example is the right to education. In Canada, few people question that children have a right to education. Nonetheless, typically, we compel children to attend school. Furthermore, as previously noted, numerous Canadian social programs such as health care and old age pensions, which are ordinarily thought to be a reflection of some sort of corresponding welfare right, are involuntary; you must contribute. The irony of a mandatory work requirement is that it promises to deliver to people more control over their lives.

The second source of scepticism about my reliance on the idea of a right to work has to do with the observation that ascribing such a right to all citizens seems to ignore the high levels of unemployment that presently exist in Canada. Few economists at present seriously believe Canada will in the near future significantly reduce its level of unemployment. The difficulty is that a right to work seems to require an economy that can achieve full employment. Note, however, that in the United States, even conservative proponents of workfare are committed implicitly to full employment.[45] Part of the point is that an advocacy of workfare does not make sense without this commitment to full employment and the belief that the costs of long-term unemployment outweigh the efficiency gains.[46] The upshot is that scepticism about the prospects for full employment are a challenge to workfare *per se*, and not just the idea of a right to work. Presumably, though, workfare proposals will not be defeated because they imply commitment to an economy with full employment. Although on theoretical grounds workfare entails a commitment to full employment, in practical terms we should not be surprised to see the implementation of workfare without the goal of full employment.

CONCLUSION

I have in this chapter argued that, while the three most common normative arguments in favour of workfare fail, the ideal of democratic citizenship can provide the normative foundations for the introduction of some workfare measures into Canadian social policy. This defence of workfare can be set in the broader context of reforming Canada's social safety net. The introduction of workfare is sometimes perceived as contrary to the fundamental moral principles that underpin our existing social policy. It is significant, however, that the normative defence of workfare advanced on democratic citizenship grounds does not require us to abandon the main pillars of our existing system of social programs — in particular, our universal system of health care, education and income support. In fact, these universal programs can also be defended on the basis of this ideal of democratic citizenship. The great virtue of these universal programs is that, in contrast to targeted social programs, they promote the citizenship we all share in a democratic society.[47] The point is that, in the course of reforming Canada's social safety net, the challenge is to envision a social policy grounded on a coherent vision of democratic citizenship where universal programs are fundamental but workfare measures can have an important place.[48]

1.   The Department of Human Resources Development explicitly endors-
      es workfare-style social policy in its discussion paper, *Improving Social
      Security in Canada* (Ottawa: Human Resources Development Canada,
      October 1994). Under one approach to reforming UI, *"Frequent
      claimants* would receive lower benefits, combined with more active
      assistance in finding a job. Income support could be conditional on
      their willingness to participate in programs that make them more
      employable" (p. 44).

2.   See, for example, Nicholas Barr, *The Economics of the Welfare State*
      (London: Weidenfeld and Nicolson, 1993), p. 100. For a recent criti-
      cal discussion of this approach to social policy, see Henry Aaron,
      Thomas Mann and Timothy Taylor (eds.), *Values and Public Policy*
      (Washington: The Brookings Institution, 1994).

3.   I have defended this general proposition at length in my recent book,
      Rights and Deprivation (Oxford: Oxford University Press, 1993), chap. 5.
      I have illustrated the practical importance of this point in the realm of
      health care. See, for example, "Justice in Health Care," in J. Burley (ed.),
      Dworkin and His Critics (Oxford: Basil Blackwell, forthcoming) and
      "Can an Egalitarian Justify Universal Access to Health Care?" (Toronto:
      manuscript, 1994).

4.   See, for example, Charles Murray, *Losing Ground: American Social Policy,
      1950-1980* (New York: Basic Books, 1984) and Lawrence Mead,
      Beyond Entitlement: The Social Obligations of Citizenship (New York: The
      Free Press, 1986).

5.   Michael Novack, *et al.*, *The New Consensus on Family and Welfare: A
      Community of Self-Reliance* (Washington: American Enterprise Institute
      for Public Policy Research, 1987).

6.   See David Ellwood, *Poor Support* (New York: Basic Books, 1988),
      pp. 179-80; Christopher Jencks, *The Homeless* (Cambridge, Mass.:
      Cambridge University Press, 1994); and Mickey Kaus, *The End of
      Equality* (New York: Basic Books, 1992).

7.   See, for example, Robert Moffitt, "Incentive Effects of the US Welfare

System: A Review," *Journal of Economic Literature*, Vol. 30, no. 1 (March 1992), pp. 1-61.

8. *The Globe and Mail*, July 11, 1994, p. A11. It is worth noting that there is significant variation among the provinces.

9. Kaus, *The End of Equality*, chap. 8.

10. Judy Darcy, "Workfare: a Bleak and Miserable Option," *The Globe and Mail*, July 1, 1994, p. A15.

11. See Jonathan Kesselman, "Work Relief Programs in the Great Depression," in J. Palmer (ed.), *Creating Jobs* (Washington: The Brookings Institution, 1978). I am grateful to Frank Swartz for drawing my attention to this example as an illustration of my claim.

12. The importance of this point I owe to a letter to *The Globe and Mail* by Errol Black, May 10, 1994, criticizing an article of mine, "Replacing Welfare with Workfare," *The Globe and Mail*, April 29, 1994.

13. This is a major theme of Judith Gueron and Edward Pauly, *From Welfare to Work* (New York: Russell Sage Foundation, 1991).

14. This has been the subject of some interesting empirical studies in the United States indicating a strong correlation between social programs that purport to track "desert" and public support of those programs. See Fay Lomax Cook and Edith J. Barrett, *Support for the American Welfare State* (New York: Columbia University Press, 1992), chap. 4; and Jeffrey A. Will, *The Deserving Poor* (New York: Garland Press, 1993), throughout. I know of no detailed comparable Canadian studies.

15. Alasdair MacIntyre, *After Virtue* (Notre Dame: University of Notre Dame Press, 1981), chap. 17.

16. J. J. C. Smart, "An Outline of a System of Utilitarian Ethics," in *Utilitarianism: For and Against* (Cambridge: Cambridge University Press, 1973).

17. John Rawls, *A Theory of Justice* (Cambridge, Mass.: Harvard University Press, 1971), pp. 310-15.

18. See, for example, David Miller, *Social Justice* (Oxford: Oxford University Press, 1976); and Michael Walzer, *Spheres of Justice* (New York: Basic Books, 1983).

19. An influential development of this theme in the context of a discussion of affirmative action is Iris Young, *Justice and the Politics of Difference* (Princeton, NJ: Princeton University Press, 1990), chap. 7.

20. I have argued this point at length in a series of articles: "Equal Opportunity and Gender Disadvantage," *The Canadian Journal of Law and Jurisprudence*, Vol. 7, no. 1 (January 1994), pp. 61-71; and "Employment Equity, Pay Equity, and Equal Opportunity," in P. Gingras (ed.), *Gender and Politics* (Toronto: Oxford University Press, forthcoming).

21. Lawrence Mead, "The New Welfare Debate: Workfare Will Transform Passive Recipients," in Beverly Fanning (ed.), *Workfare vs. Welfare* (Hudson, Wisconsin: Gem Publications, 1989), p. 61.

22. See, for example, Rawls, *A Theory of Justice*, pp. 73-75. For a broader discussion, see James Fishkin, *Justice, Equal Opportunity, and the Family* (New Haven: Yale University Press, 1983).

23. See especially Rawls, *A Theory of Justice*, pp. 72-75; and Ronald Dworkin, "What is Equality?, Part 2: Equality of Resources," *Philosophy and Public Affairs*, Vol. 10, no. 4 (Fall 1981), pp. 283-345. For influential criticisms, see Robert Nozick, *Anarchy, State, and Utopia* (New York: Basic Books, 1974), pp. 213-31; and Michael Sandel, *Liberalism and the Limits of Justice* (Cambridge: Cambridge University Press, 1982), chap. 2.

24. An argument more or less to this effect has been made by Philippe Van Parijs, "Why Surfers Should be Fed: The Liberal Case for an Unconditional Basic Income," *Philosophy and Public Affairs*, Vol. 20, no. 2 (Spring 1991), pp. 101-31. See, for a similar argument, Joseph Carens, "Compensatory Justice and Social Institutions," *Economics and Philosophy*, Vol. 1, no. 1 (April 1985), pp. 39-67.

25. In this section, I draw heavily on my discussion in *Rights and Deprivation*, pp. 197-202.

26. J. Donald Moon, "The Moral Basis of the Democratic Welfare State," in Amy Gutman (ed.), *Democracy and the Welfare State* (Princeton, NJ: Princeton University Press, 1988), p. 32.

27. Jon Elster, "Is There (or Should There Be) a Right to Work?," in Gutman (ed.), *Democracy and the Welfare State*, pp. 74-75.

28. See R. Plant, H. Lesser and P. Taylor-Gooby, *Political Philosophy and Social Welfare* (London: Routledge and Kegan-Paul, 1980), pp. 22-25.

29. See, for example, Robert Goodin, *et al.*, *Not Only the Poor: The Middle Classes and the Welfare State* (London: Allen and Unwin, 1987), chaps. 1, 5, 6, 8 and 10.

30. Michael Mandel, *The Charter of Rights and the Legalization of Politics in Canada* (Toronto: Wall and Thompson, 1989).

31. The now classic sociological statement is Robert Bellah, *et al.*, *Habits of the Heart: Individualism and Commitment in American Life* (New York: Harper and Row, 1985). The most influential philosophical statements are by Michael Sandel, *Liberalism and the Limits of Justice* (Cambridge: Cambridge University Press, 1982); "The Procedural Republic and the Unencumbered Self," *Political Theory*, Vol. 12, no. 1 (February 1984), pp. 81-96; and "Morality and the Liberal Ideal," *New Republic*, issue 190, May 7, 1984, pp. 15-17.

32. The most influential statement is Mead, *Beyond Entitlement*. See also his more recent book, *The New Politics of Poverty* (New York: Basic Books, 1992).

33. In fact, I have advanced a theory of rights, which I call the person-affecting theory of rights, that is sensitive to precisely this point. See *Rights and Deprivation*, chap. 2.

34. For some more complicated, empirical criticisms, see, for example, William Julius Wilson, *The Truly Disadvantaged* (Chicago: University of Chicago Press, 1987), pp. 159-63; and David Ellwood, *Poor Support* (New York: Basic Books, 1988), chaps. 5-6. For a partial response, see Mead, *The New Politics of Poverty*, chaps. 5-6.

35. James McCormick, *Citizens' Service, The Commission on Social Justice Issue Paper*, Vol. 10 (London: Institute for Public Policy Research, May 1994), p. 1.

36. Someone might say that, unlike the unemployed, other citizens are bearing their fair share of social responsibilities by working and paying taxes. For this reason, only the unemployed should be targeted for social programs promoting social responsibility. But, presumably, few people seriously think that only the unemployed shrug social responsibility. My point is that once this is conceded, then the case for workfare based on social responsibility is doubtful.

37. For an elaboration on this view of democracy, see my book, *The Democratic Vision of Politics* (Englewood Cliffs, N.J.: Prentice-Hall, forthcoming).

38. See the excellent analysis by Robert E. Goodin, Julian Le Grand and D.M. Gibson, "Distributional Biases in Social Service Delivery Systems," in Goodin, *et al.*, *Not Only the Poor*, pp. 127-46.

39. Maurice Roche, *Rethinking Citizenship* (Oxford: Polity Press, 1992), chap. 1; Amy Gutman, "Introduction," to Gutman (ed.), *Democracy and the Welfare State*; Desmond King and Jeremy Waldron, "Citizenship, Social Citizenship, and the Defence of Welfare Provision," *British Journal of Political Science*, Vol. 18, no. 4 (1988), pp. 413-43; and David Harris, *Justifying State Welfare* (Oxford: Basil Blackwell, 1987).

40. I have defended this view at length in *Rights and Deprivation*, pp. 41-46.

41. Murray, *Losing Ground*, p. 197.

42. See my *Rights and Deprivation*, chaps. 7-8.

43. This argument should be distinguished from the even more controversial claim that the democratic ideal is compatible only with firms that are organized around workers' control.

44. This (in my view) very sensible argument for a right to work is standardly neglected in conceptual critiques of such a right. See, for example, Jon Elster, "Is There (or Should There be) a Right to Work?," in Gutman (ed.), *Democracy and the Welfare State*.

45. Mead, *The New Politics of Poverty*, chap. 5.

46. See the excellent discussion in chapter 6 of Andrew Glyn and David Miliband (eds.), *Paying for Inequality: The Economic Cost of Social Injustice* (London: Institute for Public Policy Research/Rivers Oram Press, 1994).

47. I have defended at length the foundational importance of universality in social policy in chapter 8 of *Rights and Deprivation*.

48. I am in agreement here with the view on workfare embraced by Wilson in *The Truly Disadvantaged*, p. 163.

A L A I N   N O Ë L

THE POLITICS OF WORKFARE

INTRODUCTION

In most member countries of the Organization for Economic Co-operation and Development (OECD), the reform of social policies is currently at the top of the political agenda. This preoccupation with social policies is not new: the call for reform is almost as old as the welfare state. Still, in recent years the notion of comprehensive reform was given a new emphasis. Social policy reform moved from the sidelines to become an essential component of a country's adaptation strategy in a rapidly changing world economy.

The evolving discourse of the OECD is always revealing of policy trends. In the 1980s, the organization started to reconsider its conception of social and labour market policies. Previously seen as minor complements of economic policy, these policies became fundamental with the demise of Keynesian demand management and the rise of monetarist interpretations of unemployment. The notion of a non-accelerating or natural rate of unemployment, in particular, implied that the only lasting cure to structural unemployment would come from microeconomic reforms. It became clear in the 1980s, as explained in one OECD document, that the path to full employment went through a profound transformation of institutions, attitudes and rules, including a revision of "generous social protection."[1] With the 1990s, this monetarist emphasis on free labour markets was complemented by a new interest in active labour market policies, increasingly seen as a means of reducing unemployment, upgrading skills and increasing flexibility.[2] The OECD coined the term "active society," produced data on the respective importance of active measures (training, placement, apprenticeship *etc.*) and passive ones (cash assistance) in the different countries and called for reforms that would reshape the welfare state, labour markets and even society.[3]

The new discourse of the OECD appears disarmingly simple, and particularly ambivalent. According to a much-discussed 1994 report, large-scale unemployment in Europe, Canada and Australia, as well as the proliferation of bad jobs and the rise of unemployment in the United States, have "the same root cause: the failure to adapt satisfactorily to change." A revision of all social policies is thus essential, to see "where, and to what extent, each may have contributed to ossifying the capacity of economies and the will of societies to adapt," and to find "how to remove those disincentives without harming the degree of social protection that it is each society's wish to provide." With such vague and potentially conflicting objectives, it is hardly surprising that the OECD sees social policy reform as "a daunting task."[4]

The aims of social policy reform are anything but clear. In Canada, for instance, the call for reform is primarily justified by the claim that the social safety net is outdated and unable to face new challenges.[5] But what does this diagnosis mean? What are the choices reform entails? What are the principles at stake? If choices have to be made among equity, budgetary concerns, labour market flexibility and levels of employment, what objectives should prevail? More fundamentally, what exactly is a country's capacity "to adapt satisfactorily to change?"

Work-for-welfare proposals are a case in point. Workfare, here, is understood in its broadest sense as the replacement of "income support alone...by a combination of active reintegration policies, positive incentives to search for work and a safety net in the form of minimum income security."[6] When comprehensive social policy reforms are considered, in Canada or elsewhere, workfare proposals are almost always put forward because they establish a link between income support measures and the labour market, and constitute a crucial element in the shift from passive to active labour market policies. The objectives of work-for-welfare measures, however, appear ambiguous. Often sold as a measure to reduce the welfare dependency of the long-term unemployed, they are also presented as a deterrent to discourage "undeserving" welfare applicants, as a means of reducing social expenditures or as an active labour market policy with the potential to foster an upgrading in skills and a reduction in unemployment. The problem is that these different objectives are unlikely to be met simultaneously. Making effective welfare-to-work programs widely available, for instance, is costly. Wrongly convinced that workfare leads to lower expenditures, "the enthusiastic public has not had to weigh its interest in making welfare mothers work against its eagerness to pay the bill."[7] Such tensions between contradictory objectives underline the political dimension of workfare proposals and, by extension, of social policy reform. Yet, most of the literature deals with the technical or economic dimensions of reform.

The aim of this chapter is to clarify the political meaning of work-for-welfare proposals by identifying and assessing the different rationales offered to support reform. In this chapter, I seek to establish three arguments: first, many rationales are offered for workfare, but the number of possible justifications can be reduced to a few, not all of them being well founded or convincing; second, the arguments that prevail in the end will vary in time and across countries but are likely to reflect the type of welfare state institutions a country has inherited from its past; and third, in a liberal welfare state such as Canada, workfare programs are likely to be under-funded, inefficient and probably self-defeating, but they could also be part of a new, more European orientation in social policy.

Clarifying the rationale for work-for-welfare proposals will not yield definite conclusions about their feasibility, cost or efficiency. The exercise should lead nevertheless to a better understanding of the principles underlying welfare reform. Writing about education policy, Amy Gutman argues that "all significant policy prescriptions presuppose...a political theory of the proper role of government" and concludes that we cannot make or consider proposals "without exposing our principles and investigating their implications."[8] With work-for-welfare, the issues at stake appear particularly unclear. Workfare tends to oppose the right and the left, but even these battle lines are not clearly drawn. In this chapter, it is suggested there are in fact definite dimensions to this political debate: an understanding of these dimensions can help evaluate the relevance, the legitimacy and the political viability of workfare proposals and, more generally, of social policy reform.

ARGUMENTS FOR WORKFARE

Why do governments promote and adopt workfare measures? While an exhaustive list of reasons is probably out of reach, I think most arguments and motivations can be associated with four objectives. In a nutshell, workfare can be advocated to influence welfare beneficiaries, to improve the supply of labour, to meet budgetary constraints or to respond to the demands of voters.

Influencing Beneficiaries

Consider, first, workfare as a means of influencing welfare recipients. Traditionally, various forms of work or residence requirements were used to determine whether individuals demanding relief were "deserving" or not. In 1915, for instance, Toronto's House of Industry required men seeking help "to break up a crate of rocks weighing 650 pounds."[9] The idea was less to change individuals seeking help than to deter those who could be tempted to take advantage of whatever support was offered. With the administration of means tests, harsh screening practices lost their importance. In the 1960s and 1970s, countries such as Canada and the United States largely based public assistance on need and did not invest much to encourage welfare recipients to work, on the assumption that poverty was essentially marginal or temporary.[10] The debate on work and welfare resurfaced in the 1980s, in the US in particular, with the publication of Charles Murray's *Losing Ground*. Social assistance programs, argued Murray, were themselves a major cause not only of chronic poverty, but also of unemployment, female-headed families, falling educational achievements and crime. Programs intended to help recipients gave them the wrong incentives and trapped many into "dependency."[11] In his 1986 State of the Union address, Ronald Reagan placed the problem of welfare dependency on the agenda and announced reforms that involved work requirements for welfare recipients.[12] Eight years later, Bill Clinton reiterated the argument when he proposed to "end welfare as we know it" and "to change it from a system based on dependence to a system that works toward independence...so that the focus is clearly on work."[13] In Canada, Lloyd Axworthy, minister of Human Resources

Development, echoed the same theme when he stated that social security programs should be reformed "to create hope and end dependency."[14]

For all its political salience, the "dependency" argument appears problematic on many counts. First, it is not obvious that income security generates dependency. Studies on the incentive effects of the welfare system do indicate that welfare participation is "an economic decision based on labour supply considerations" and is therefore influenced by expected wages, the level of benefits, the implicit welfare tax rate and "nonmonetary inhibiting factors such as stigma."[15] The structure of economic incentives, however, may be acknowledged by the individuals concerned without affecting the labour market behaviour of others.[16] In other words, while most people who are eligible become participants — as we should expect with any "economic decision" — the evidence indicates that those who are not eligible are unlikely to change their labour market situation to become eligible. This implies, according to Robert Moffitt, that "the problem of welfare 'dependency' (i.e., participation in AFDC [Aid to Families with Dependent Children]) cannot be ascribed to the work disincentives of the program."[17] Changes are in fact more likely in the reverse direction: while very few individuals willingly deteriorate their labour market situation, large numbers do leave welfare for the labour market, in spite of poor work incentives.[18] Overall, the evolution of the welfare caseload has much less to do with policy-induced incentives than with the employment situation.[19] An empirical test for the Canadian provinces between 1977 and 1982 confirms that the rise in the number of social assistance beneficiaries is not related to changes in the structure of incentives, but can be explained by the unemployment situation.[20]

Even if dependency were a problem, work requirements might not be the best tools to attack it. While it is beyond the scope of this chapter to review accumulated evidence, I would like to stress that, at best, the impact of work requirements on welfare participation is small. Recent studies tend to identify modest, positive impacts on employment and earnings, and marginal effects on welfare caseloads and expenditures.[21] Income gains, however, are too small to lift participants and their families out of poverty.[22] As for employment gains, they seem just as limited and could well be cancelled at the macroeconomic level: a job obtained by someone on welfare could well be a job lost for someone in the market.[23] Apparently, such displacement effects are quite important when programs are not targeted precisely toward specific groups.[24] Programs perceived as helpful could also attract more and better qualified people to welfare and delay their exit, thus offsetting the savings associated with positive results.[25] Overall, workfare programs may succeed in influencing beneficiaries and they may even be worthwhile for some of those involved but, short of massive investments, they are unlikely to make a long-term difference.[26] "How can one expect," concludes Lars Osberg, "that high unemployment, year after year, will not generate more long-term dependence on social assistance?"[27]

Given these lacklustre perspectives, the notion that workfare can usefully influence welfare recipients could be considered simply invalid. Some conclude that, indeed, workfare is best understood as an ideology.[28] Other arguments can, however, supplement or, to some extent, shore up the dependency argument. First, proponents of workfare can fall back on the old deterrence argument. Second, they can claim modest results are better than none. Third, they can argue that an approach that is fair is justified even if inefficient.

The deterrence argument is almost as ubiquitous as its dependency counterpart. In this perspective, workfare must be evaluated not only for what it does to participants, but also for its capacity to discourage "undeserving" welfare claimants.[29] Work incentives, explained André Bourbeau, then Quebec minister in charge of income security, had an impact on Quebec society: "a certain number of persons realized that, all things considered, it remained more advantageous to keep one's job than to depend on income security."[30] This deterrence argument is contradicted by the studies presented above. At the micro level, there is no evidence that "undeserving" individuals willingly modify their labour market situation to become eligible for social assistance. Macroeconomic analyses confirm these results by identifying the strong and significant link between the employment situation and the number of people on welfare.[31] Theoretically, for deterrence to be effective, the work demanded for welfare would have to be quite stringent, "considerably in excess of that which poor individuals would do in the absence of intervention," and probably beyond what would be seen as fair and reasonable.[32]

Even if we accept that workfare programs are unlikely to deter work avoidance and may not have more than limited, local impacts, one could still argue that modest results are better than none. This seems to be the position of the OECD and of many American policy analysts, and, on the face of it, it seems incontrovertible.[33] A few *caveats* are nevertheless in order. First, achieving such modest results may be costly and it remains far from certain that the operation could yield net gains for society.[34] Second, workfare measures have often been introduced in a context of hostility toward welfare recipients. In both Canada and the United States, work-for-welfare proposals tend to be accompanied by a discourse on fraud and abuse that denigrates people on welfare. If the modest employment and earnings gains of a few participants are obtained at the expense of increased stigma for the rest, the outcome can hardly be satisfactory. Stigma is likely to make an exit from welfare more difficult, and it could increase social isolation, which Wilson sees as crucial in explaining inner-city problems.[35] Finally, the modest gains expected from workfare risk being oversold to the public, a situation which in due time could create disappointment and undermine the support for welfare and for training programs.[36] To conclude, the limited benefits associated with workfare could come at a price that cannot be measured solely in budgetary terms.

The idea of influencing beneficiaries is central to political debates on workfare less because it is a tried and true idea than because it is in tune with the type of liberalism that prevails in North America. In the United States, writes William Julius Wilson, poverty has primarily been understood as an individual rather than a social problem, and solutions naturally focus on individual characteristics.[37] The understanding that underlies arguments in terms of incentives or mandated participation is so powerful that many are ready to accept it despite a lack of evidence. "Even in the absence of a strong economic rationale," argues Ailee Moon, "workfare may be preferred if it fits with the nation's social values and improves equity or perceived fairness of the welfare system."[38] Without workfare, adds Robert Pruger, AFDC would lack legitimacy.[39] The question, as we will see below, is how far citizens and governments are willing to go to uphold these values and principles.

Influencing the Labour Market

The objectives put forward by the OECD concern less welfare recipients than the overall state of the labour market in member countries. Social policy reform in this perspective, and by extension work-for-welfare, is promoted because it can facilitate adjustment and make the labour market more flexible. Influencing beneficiaries is less important than influencing the labour market. In other words, the aim is less to alter the behaviour of individuals held responsible for their situation than to alter and broaden the opportunities these individuals may face in the labour market. The key words are not dependency and deterrence, but rather active labour market policies, flexibility and reintegration.[40]

Insofar as the dependency and deterrence arguments for work-for-welfare measures appear unconvincing, it may seem that labour market arguments will not be valid either. In North America, at least, the impact of work-for-welfare measures on labour markets is limited because "labour supply elasticities are typically quite small," that is to say that the incentives associated with social assistance or workfare do not have an important impact.[41] One may also question the idea that this type of investment in human resources is critical for growth, equity and employment. It is not certain, for instance, that a shortage of skills or a lack of labour market preparation lie behind the rise of unemployment and inequality in North America.[42]

In continental Europe, however, arguments about work-for-welfare are not defined primarily in microeconomic, labour supply terms. Systematic, experimental policy evaluations, for instance, have not been considered critical.[43] Work-for-welfare measures are deemed relevant less for their potential effects on individuals than for their fit within a broader framework of policies and institutions. What stands as workfare is associated with a package of measures that make the labour market flexible, flexibility being understood less as the "static" (or defensive) freedom to hire and fire and to pay low wages, than as the "dynamic" (or offensive) capacity to negotiate change, upgrade skills and improve productivity.[44] Work-for-welfare is also understood as a social measure aimed at reintegrating individuals and groups excluded from the labour market.

Following the OECD, we can take Sweden as the polar opposite of the US. Between these two countries, an opposition in labour market policies can be traced back at least to the 1960s. Whereas the American government gave a marginal role to such policies, Sweden understood them as critical to structure the labour market so that full employment could be maintained without inflation.[45] A range of measures were adopted to train the unemployed or keep them in or close to the labour market. Swedish labour market policies assume it is better to provide training grants, mobility assistance, rehabilitation measures or even subsidized temporary work than to simply hand out cash assistance.[46] Most of these measures can be associated with the North American notion of work-for-welfare, because the unemployed have to accept "suitable work" or training programs to maintain their benefits, and because the "rules about job refusals are not mere formalities."[47]

Between 1990 and 1994, Sweden was the OECD country that spent the most, as a percentage of Gross Domestic Product (GDP), on such active labour market policies. The country was also unique in spending much more on active than on passive measures, except in 1993-94, when a severe recession raised the cost of income support above that of active measures. Even then, active measures remained a priority: while cash-assistance conditions were restricted, the active labour market program was "radically expanded."[48] Again, because "efficiency aspects have had second-order priority to equity considerations," these measures have not been evaluated extensively. Still, most observers agree they help account for the country's "successful unemployment record" up to 1992.[49] Because they facilitated geographical and job mobility, active labour market policies gave Sweden what was deemed as the most flexible labour market in the OECD, even with high employment levels, high wages and generous unemployment benefits.[50]

In Germany, a country that stands between the United States and Sweden in terms of active labour market expenditures, arguments justifying labour market policies are similar to those in Sweden. In fact, the evolution of German policies was influenced by Swedish innovations, as well as by the country's traditional emphasis on employment policy and on self-administration by unions and employers. As in Sweden, German policies stress working-class rather than individual issues, work and wages rather than deviance and poverty and adjustment and qualifications rather than deterrence and dependency. The core purpose of labour market policies is to provide the unemployed with placement, training and temporary work opportunities, and to keep pure income support as a last resort.[51]

The French case represents a third variant of the labour market argument for work-for-welfare. Less committed to intervention than Germany, the country has neither the social democratic nor the neo-corporatist tradition that would make comprehensive employment policies possible. Still, the problem of unemployment is understood in social more than in individual terms. The recent debate on the *revenu minimum d'insertion*, for instance, made clear that the problem of long-term unemployment was a labour market problem and called for more than individual incentives. The very notion of *insertion* — or reintegration — underlines the need to include citizens who are perceived as victims of labour market processes about which they cannot do much. A French reintegration "contract" — through which a beneficiary seeks to change his or her situation through various means (including training and temporary work, but also medical treatments and professional help) is only marginally understood in terms of incentives, and it may leave an individual fairly remote from the labour market. The priority of French work-for-welfare measures is the re-establishment of meaningful social links.[52]

Labour market arguments for workfare cannot be assessed as easily as individual arguments. The ties established between social assistance and the labour market are not designed merely to bring individuals back to the labour market, but also to institutionalize rules that facilitate dynamic (or offensive) labour market flexibility and that embody a certain understanding of solidarity. Success is thus measured less in terms of costs and benefits than in terms of employment and equity. More elusive, such notions nevertheless allow positive evaluations.[53] To a large extent, it is the success of active labour market policies of the type implemented in continental Europe that has led the OECD to affirm their importance and to call for social policy reforms.

Labour market arguments, however, are not without their own limitations. First, it is far from certain that current unemployment problems are related to flexibility or to labour market rigidities, and work-welfare links may not be as critical as expected.[54] Second, as with individual-based workfare proposals, labour market approaches face important budgetary constraints. The French experience with reintegration, for instance, is limited by a lack of resources; a large proportion of beneficiaries fail to obtain reintegration contracts or must accept contracts of little labour market relevance.[55] Finally, a tension also exists, in particular in the most interventionist countries, between labour market aims and the preservation of individual autonomy. The extensive Swedish labour market policies, in particular, run the risk of denying choices to individuals. "However rational from an economic as well as an individual standpoint," writes Bo Rothstein, "and however morally acceptable a solution is to the problem of unemployment, active labour market policy unavoidably contains strong elements of paternalism."[56]

Reducing the Social Budget

A third set of arguments for workfare concern budgetary objectives. Often associated with the dependency/deterrence arguments, this type of argument suggests important economies can be achieved with workfare, through reductions in the number of beneficiaries. As mentioned above, unless major investments are accepted — to make workfare an extensive measure — such savings are likely to be minor, if not marginal. A genuine commitment to transform welfare "as we know it" would in fact be expensive, at least in the short and medium term.

Insofar as the most ambitious active labour market policies are successful, there is theoretically a tradeoff with passive, purely redistributive policies. Investments in workfare should eventually reduce income security expenditures. Countries committed to active policies, however, often spend a great deal on passive measures. Their commitment to labour market programs may be combined with generous compensation for unemployment, just as low levels of expenditures may coexist in both areas (in the US for instance).[57] Consequently, even the most comprehensive active labour market policies may not be counter-balanced by savings in passive measures.

The implementation of workfare measures, however, may not be neutral with respect to benefits. Social assistance reforms often provide an occasion for reducing the level of benefits received by large categories of the population. In the US, for instance, AFDC benefits were "seriously eroded by inflation" in the 1970-1992 period, just as a variety of workfare measures were introduced.[58] Likewise, in the Canadian provinces, the reform of social assistance has often meant reducing the benefits of those deemed able to work. In the process, some beneficiaries have seen their income increase but, overall, welfare benefits fell in real terms (between 1986 and 1991).[59] The link between lower benefits and workfare is nowhere clearer than in the reform proposals issued by the Canadian government in October 1994. A new category would be created for frequent unemployment insurance claimants, who not only would be expected to participate in employment development programs, but also would receive benefits that could be lower, of a different duration or based on an income test. As with the Quebec social assistance reform of 1988, work-for-welfare measures are in this case associated with lower benefits for participants and potential participants.[60]

If work-for-welfare measures are accompanied by significant benefit reductions, the budgetary savings associated with reform may be more important than what is suggested by cost-and-benefit studies. In this case, however, the issue is no longer one of efficiency. It concerns distribution. Reform becomes motivated not by the need to return beneficiaries to the labour market, but rather by the simple idea that social assistance should be less generous. According to Gordon Lafer, the Reagan and Bush administrations in the US used work-for-welfare and training in this perspective, primarily to legitimate "deep cuts in social welfare benefits."[61] The fact is that while workfare measures yielded no more than modest results, changes in the income distribution proved highly significant: between 1979 and 1986, the US poverty rate increased by 2.6 points, basically because of contractions in transfer programs.[62]

Workfare proposals are often components of broader agendas that include social assistance cutbacks. Arguments for workfare, however, should not be confused with arguments for lower and more selective benefits. If work-for-welfare is to mean something, it must be valuable in itself, in terms of reduced caseloads, labour market integration or costs and benefits. If the aim is simply to lower transfers to the poor, arguments in favour of work-for-welfare should not be relevant. There is no evidence that less generous social transfers have microeconomic or macroeconomic benefits in terms of efficiency.[63] Once again, the question in this case is purely one of distribution.

To sum up, workfare proposals are often accompanied by reductions in benefits, but budgetary arguments for workfare must make sense on their own, because such cutbacks are basically unrelated to the efficiency or to the costs and benefits of workfare. In themselves, budgetary considerations justify neither limited nor extensive measures. Truly effective work-for-welfare measures are likely to increase, not reduce, social spending.

Responding to Voters' Demands

It has already been suggested that workfare and active labour market policies have a lot to do with principles, values, traditions and institutions. It could be argued that workfare is simply something voters demand in liberal democracies. Irrespective of the findings of various studies and budgetary implications, the argument for workfare would be fundamentally political. Apparently, the Ontario government based its recent reform of welfare controls on focus groups indicating that

Ontarians wanted tighter controls as a matter of principle, even though such controls were likely to be ineffective in reducing costs.[64]

One interpretation would stress the self-interested rationality of the median voter, who would dislike redistribution and prefer to associate it with strict measures. Such an interpretation does not hold, however, if the median voter has egalitarian or social democratic preferences.[65] More fundamentally, the very existence of social programs and their enduring legitimacy suggest self-interest is not the primary determinant of choice when major policy options are considered. Because electoral outcomes are "detached" from individual votes, argue Brennan and Lomasky, "the considerations that predominate in market choice cannot be presumed to predominate in electoral choice." Choosing an option at the ballot box is not, contrary to what happens in the market, "decisive"; it may not produce the chosen outcome. As a consequence, values and principles — the quest for "truth" and "justice" — play an important role in political debates.[66]

What are the principles involved in workfare? More precisely, what are the principles voters consider important when thinking about workfare? The question is complex and would deserve a lengthy discussion. What can at least be said is that liberal societies display a commitment to a minimum level of welfare for all citizens, accompanied by some form of guarantee that transfers to the poor are not entirely unconditional.[67] Even in the US, where the welfare state appears least entrenched, citizens approve of income support for the poor, especially if they perceive existing programs as effective and restricted to "deserving" recipients.[68] Minimum incomes, however, are not sufficient. According to sociologist Robert E. Lane, a number of empirical studies concur to show "that working activities are the best agents of well-being and the best sources of cognitive development, a sense of personal control, and self-esteem available in economic life, better than a higher standard of living, and, I believe, better than what is offered by leisure."[69] In a democracy, work serves as a testimony that a person is an autonomous, equal and independent agent able to participate in the community. This is why, notes J. Donald Moon, "to exercise one's right to welfare is, in American society, a sign of failure."[70] Work in itself, apart from income, thus occupies a central place in liberal democracies.[71] Combined with a commitment to maintain incomes for the poorest, the importance granted to work creates a tension that is nowhere more obvious than in discussions of workfare.

The interest in workfare is indeed sustained by these two opposing values. On one hand, workfare appeals to the idea of control that emerges once unconditional transfers to the poor are rejected. The theoretical foundation here is best provided by neo-classical economics and the notion of work as a negative utility. On the other hand, workfare also appears as a means to make excluded individuals full participants, as a way to help citizens achieve self-respect and autonomy. Here, of course, the main theoretical inspiration can be found in Marx, where work is the primary source of self-realization.[72] With such foundations, it is not surprising that work-for-welfare measures draw the attention of both the right and the left, and that variants can be found in social democratic Sweden as well as in Thatcher's Britain.

We have surveyed thus far the different rationales that have been given to justify workfare. These arguments have had varying weight in the different countries of the OECD and they have given rise to different institutions. In part, these differences can be associated with the left-right tension just identified. The full picture, however, is more complex. There are, in the OECD, three types of workfare models, each one involving a specific policy dilemma.

THE THREE WORLDS OF WORKFARE

Welfare states are often understood in terms of more or less: more or less generous, advanced, interventionist *etc.* Beyond these dimensions, however, welfare institutions also differ in kind. For voters, the notions of citizenship and solidarity embodied in welfare programs are in fact likely to matter more than degrees of intervention or levels of expenditure. Are programs universal, selective or means-tested? Are benefits determined by contributions? Is access administered by bureaucrats, trade unions or local communities?

To make sense of such variations, Gøsta Esping-Andersen has classified the various welfare states of the OECD into three ideal-typical categories. First, comes the conservative welfare state, established to a large extent from above, by governments bent on preserving the social and political *status quo* in the face of rapid economic change. The German welfare state, for instance, has its origins in Bismarck's attempt to undermine the Social Democrats. The idea was less to counter market failures or to institutionalize new rights than to protect existing social groups. A variety of social protection schemes was instituted, each one designed for a particular category of the population. Committed to spend, conservative welfare states do so in a particular manner, through various corporatist and differentiated mechanisms. For social assistance and labour market policies, this implies a strong reliance on labour market actors and, as a consequence, an emphasis on work and skills. Second comes the liberal welfare state, which best mirrors the market logic and is typical of Anglo-Saxon democracies. In this case, social protection combines two mechanisms: market or state-supported insurance to protect the majority against various risks, and means-tested assistance for those unable or unwilling to insure themselves against risk. As a last recourse, social assistance is granted reluctantly, when the poor can prove they are deserving. The recourse to assistance is seen as an individual, often temporary, problem. Finally, Esping-Andersen identifies social democratic welfare states, where social protection is defined in terms of rights and is to a large extent provided through universal programs. An outcome of social democracy, this last type of welfare state is not only the most generous, but also the most positive about social programs, seen less as a reluctantly accepted necessity than as a celebrated expression of a shared sense of citizenship.[73]

The relative importance of active labour market policies (involving training and employment measures) *versus* passive policies (income support) is clearly related to Esping-Andersen's welfare state types. In a cross-sectional analysis of expenditures, Thomas Janoski finds that social democratic welfare states are strongly and positively correlated with active expenditures as a percentage of GDP, liberal welfare states are negatively correlated and conservative welfare states are weakly and positively correlated. Sweden, for instance, makes an extensive use of active policies and does so in a counter-cyclical manner, whereas the US spends less, and does so less in response to business cycles than to demographic and partisan pressures. In between, German expenditures appear determined primarily by the rise of unemployment and by the power of the left.[74] The differences, however, go much beyond levels and determinants of expenditures. The rationales for active labour market policies, and by extension for workfare, vary with regime types.

In the previous section, four types of arguments were presented: workfare was justified in turn by its impact on beneficiaries, on labour markets, on social budgets and on voters. These different arguments were not always convincing, but they nevertheless proved relevant politically. More precisely, these various arguments point to key differences in North American and European debates. Whereas dependency is at the core of the American discussion on workfare, the search for labour market flexibility stands at the forefront in Europe. Distinctions among welfare regimes help us make sense of these differences. Indeed, the dependency argument is not so much North American as it is anchored in the liberal conception of the welfare state. Likewise, labour market arguments are typical of conservative and social democratic welfare states.

Liberal welfare states deal with long-term unemployment and poverty primarily through social assistance, a residual program targeted at those who are unable to provide for themselves through work, savings or insurance. The selective nature of assistance implies it must be based on means tests. In itself, this reliance on individual tests makes workfare congenial. Imposed work is after all one of the oldest methods used to test recipients' desert. In addition, the liberal, individualist understanding of poverty encourages the search for solutions that affect individual behaviour. In this respect, workfare also appears promising. At the same time, liberal welfare states are also characterized by their reluctance to spend, and they may not invest much in workfare, even though the approach is perceived as useful. Here lies the fundamental dilemma of workfare in liberal welfare states: the approach appears valuable but its implementation is constrained by cost considerations.

Conservative welfare states face a somewhat similar dilemma: useful to facilitate labour market adjustments or to reintegrate excluded individuals, workfare measures are sufficiently expensive not to be fully deployed. Contrary to the liberal welfare states, the conservative ones give a broader dimension to social programs, which tend to be associated with categories of the population rather than with individuals. In Germany, for instance, civil servants have programs of their own and do not contribute to the *Bundesanstalt* (Federal Institute of Labour Placement and Unemployment Compensation).[75] In France, a series of programs protect various categories of the population (the aged, the handicapped, single mothers, the long-term unemployed *etc.*); the *revenu minimum d'insertion* was only added in 1988, to patch the remaining holes in the safety net.[76] Allocated to various categories, income support and social services are an object of constant arbitration. Hence, the will to improve skills and to facilitate adjustment tends to be counterbalanced by various redistribution priorities. The adjustment-spending dilemma thus defines most debates on labour market policies.[77]

Because they have had more success in remaining near full-employment and are also more committed to active labour market policies, social democratic welfare states largely escaped the workfare *versus* budget dilemmas of liberal and conservative states. Spending was not a central issue. Even with rising unemployment rates, budgetary constraints do not undermine labour market policies because these policies are understood as counter-cyclical instruments and are institutionalized as such.[78] The primary social democratic dilemma concerns, instead, the delicate equilibrium to be maintained between labour market objectives and the preservation of individual autonomy. With most social programs, social democracy combines generous transfers with distant interventions: universality disconnects redistribution from individual characteristics. Labour market interventions, however, have a strong individual component and even carry an element of compulsion, especially when few unemployed are faced with numerous programs and opportunities. To counter this dilemma, social democrats have given an important role to trade unions in the administration of labour market programs.[79] The difficulty nevertheless remains significant.

The figure on page 56 puts together the different arguments for workfare, in a pattern that suggests there are essentially three basic ideas at stake, ideas that are combined differently according to the type of welfare institutions a given country inherited from its past.[80]

Overall, liberal welfare states give little importance to labour market adjustment or reintegration. They care much, however, about the motivations of individuals receiving assistance, and see workfare as a valuable tool to influence these motivations. At the same time, the low priority given to social assistance prevents liberal states from investing enough to transform "welfare as we know it." The result is the liberal dilemma, a tension between ambitious, regularly stated behavioural objectives and reluctant budgetary commitments.[81] Given the political difficulty of designing and adopting comprehensive welfare reform, the most likely outcome is a modest effort at implementing workfare, an effort that will be, at best, effective for only a few and, at worst, useless and self-defeating. This, deplores Judith M. Gueron, is "welfare reform as usual: an underfunded nation-wide program, limited real change, unanswered questions about the potential for success, and a further disillusioned public."[82]

Figure
The Three Dilemmas of Workfare

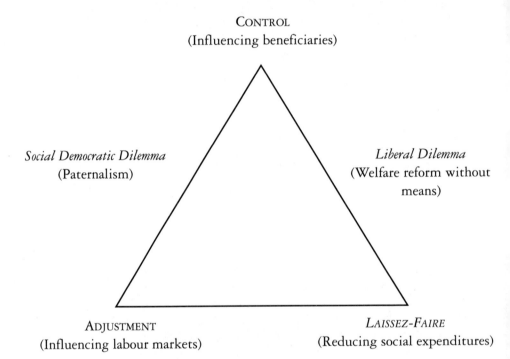

CONTROL
(Influencing beneficiaries)

Social Democratic Dilemma
(Paternalism)

Liberal Dilemma
(Welfare reform without means)

ADJUSTMENT
(Influencing labour markets)

LAISSEZ-FAIRE
(Reducing social expenditures)

Conservative Dilemma
(Partial commitment to active labour market policies)

The dilemma of conservative welfare states is also expressed by a lack of funding that leaves many claimants without access to existing programs. In France, for instance, integration contracts are not available to all those concerned. In Germany, the same tension is institutionalized in the *Bundesanstalt's* contradictory roles: responsible for both retraining and unemployment benefits, the federal labour institute sees its capacity to pursue active policies curtailed by the rise of passive expenditures, precisely when active policies are most needed, in periods of high unemployment ("unless the federal government itself is prepared to finance the crisis-induced additional expenditures").[83] This tension between adjustment and budgetary objectives also translates into a tendency, typical of conservative welfare states, to limit the most helpful programs to specific categories of the population, thus creating labour markets that may be flexible but remain segmented.[84]

While cost necessarily remains a concern, social democratic welfare states escape to a large extent these dilemmas because labour market expenditures tend to be institutionalized as entitlements. They face a dilemma of their own, however, characterized earlier as a tension between interventionism and paternalism. Of the three dilemmas, this is certainly the least problematic, considering that many universal programs counter-balance the potential pressures put on individuals by labour market policies.[85] Still, there is a sense in which the active search for labour market flexibility combined with intensive and individualized services for the unemployed can lead to a lack of control, a "black hole" in democracy. Dependency, here, takes a new meaning, but is no less problematic.[86] The solution seems to be the reintroduction of choice and autonomy within welfare institutions. It also hinges on the creation of new political alignments that would reflect the new, post-industrial character of social democratic societies.[87]

To sum up, arguments about workfare abound and they vary with the types of welfare states the different countries have institutionalized, but they can be captured in three interrelated dilemmas. Liberal states hesitate between control and *laissez-faire*, conservative states between *laissez-faire* and adjustment and social democratic states between adjustment and control. For a country such as Canada, a liberal welfare state that incorporates some social democratic and conservative elements, this pattern is not without implications.

DEBATING WORKFARE IN CANADA

Like most countries, Canada does not constitute a pure type of welfare state. Essentially liberal, the Canadian welfare state gives priority to market mechanisms, especially for the provision of income security. At the same time, Canadian institutions embody elements of the universalism typical of social democratic welfare states, as well as a few conservative features. Social preoccupations less related to the labour market, in particular, can be met with social democratic, universal programs — health care and education, for example. In income security, there are also conservative elements: the family, for instance, is often privileged.[88] Overall, however, labour market failures are compensated by insurance or means-tested programs.[89] This reliance on liberal solutions for labour market issues suggests that Canadian debates on workfare are likely to be liberal debates. In Canada, welfare dependency, deterrence and budget constraints are the key concepts invoked by politicians when discussing workfare or welfare reform. Typically, the major failure of workfare measures already in place rests in their incapacity to accommodate all willing participants. In Quebec, for instance, almost 50,000 adult welfare recipients are available and waiting to participate in welfare employability programs.[90]

At the same time, Canada is not exactly like the US. Income support is less restrictive, more generous and complemented by universal measures such as medicare that improve the situation of the poorest. Mandatory workfare is also deemed unacceptable.[91] According to Patricia Evans, these differences explain why Canadian discussions on workfare have focussed more on the notion of a social contract than on strict work requirements. As she recognizes, however, the same notion of contract now prevails in the US.[92] The key difference, in my opinion, is that the more generous dimensions of the Canadian welfare state introduce a dualistic pattern into the work-for-welfare debate. In other words, the conservative and social democratic elements in Canada's welfare state make it possible to discuss workfare in the terms of the conservative discourse, without however abandoning the liberal argumentation.

Consider the current discussion on training and employability. Throughout Canada, there is a growing consensus that investment in training is imperative to create the skilled workforce necessary for the country to remain competitive. New institutions have been created that bring trade unions, business and governments together, to co-operate in the promotion and support of labour market training.[93] These institutions, however, exclude the unemployed. In Quebec, for instance, this exclusion is explicit and rationalized: "It does not seem a good idea," explains Quebec's policy paper on training, "to make the *Société québécoise de développement de la main-d'oeuvre* (the province's labour market training board) responsible for programs aimed at the development of employability...a board managed by labour market partners cannot have the responsibility for social programs."[94]

The Quebec government thus defines two tracks linking individuals to the labour market: training for those who are employed, most likely in companies that provide stable employment and are unionized; and employability development for the unemployed, those who have little labour market prospects other than unskilled, precarious jobs at the bottom of the scale.[95] These two tracks are managed differently, concern different individuals (and often different genders), and rarely ever cross. They are in fact so distinct that standard working conditions do not even apply to the participants of some employability programs.

In their work on the politics of old-age income security in Canada, John Myles and Les Teichroew identify two distinct policy spheres. On one hand, there is the public politics of poverty and the Guaranteed Income Supplement for the elderly with low incomes. On the other, they find the semi-private politics of corporate welfare, where pensions are subsidized by the state but remain private, and largely defined through business-labour negotiations. The two spheres concern different individuals — and to some extent different genders — and remain largely unconnected. Often seen as a motherhood political issue, pensions are in fact a divisive issue: a dualistic welfare state acknowledges and reinforces the existing polarization of incomes and situations.[96]

With respect to training and workfare, a similar dualistic pattern is emerging, with tripartite training arrangements on one hand, and imposed employability measures on the other. Behind a unanimous rhetoric stressing education, skills and competitiveness, there are in fact two discourses. The first, on training, refers to European discussions on labour market adjustment, and evokes images of a high value-added economy. The second, on employability and workfare, has American references and appeals to those who worry about welfare fraud and dependency. Hence, two of the three logical dilemmas identified above co-exist within the Canadian welfare state. This dualism may be most obvious in Quebec, but it is present in the rest of the country as well. With its proposal to create a distinct unemployment insurance regime for frequent claimants, the federal government appears in tune with this dual logic.

Given the predominantly liberal character of the Canadian welfare state, the liberal logic of control and employability should prevail when it conflicts with the conservative/adjustment understanding of labour market policy. A decreased emphasis on the logic of employability, however, cannot be excluded. In 1982, the Quebec government took income security out of the Ministry of Social Affairs, to create the Ministry of Manpower and Income Security. The logic behind the move was quite clear and reflected the social democratic views of the minister, Pierre Marois. Income security, the government argued, was meant to provide a basic income for those unable to work, but it was also intended to "allow the largest number to acquire autonomy through sufficiently paid work." Income security, integration into the workplace and training were all tied and could not be promoted in isolation.[97] Integration was then the key word with respect to work and welfare: in contrast to employability, the concept suggested unemployment and poverty were rooted in labour market, not personal, deficiencies. In the following years, the Quebec government moved away from this labour market perspective, to adopt a punitive discourse toward welfare recipients.[98] In 1994, Premier Daniel Johnson — who is on the right of the Quebec political spectrum — sealed this reorientation by creating a Ministry of Income Security distinct from the new Ministry of Employment, in charge among other things of training programs.[99] This latest move demonstrated the enduring weight of liberalism in Canadian conceptions of workfare. It also indicated, however, that a space remained open for alternative, more European conceptions.[100]

CONCLUSION

The politics of workfare easily gives rise to excessive rhetoric. Welfare recipients are accused of abusing generous programs, voters are perceived as alienated and critical of the welfare state and governments are suspected of imposing harsh, unfair and useless treatments. In fact, fraud and abuse are essentially marginal, voters tend to support means-tested and welfare programs in general and workfare measures are usually complex sets of programs meant to facilitate the transition toward the labour market. Workfare programs also tend to apply to limited numbers of recipients, they succeed for an even smaller minority and they have little impact on poverty, unemployment and social expenditures.

In this chapter, I have attempted to identify the main arguments used to justify workfare, and found that there were in fact no more than a few arguments, not all of them supported by convincing evidence. In a nutshell, work-for-welfare measures can be advocated as forms of control, as labour market interventions, as methods to reduce expenditures or as politically popular decisions. As a form of control, workfare concerns mostly the behaviour of individuals; it may or may not prove successful at this microeconomic level, but it does not yield the expected benefits at the macroeconomic level, unless significant resources are committed to influence welfare recipients. As a means to facilitate labour market adjustment and social integration, workfare appears more useful, insofar as it is associated with a coherent series of labour market policies. Again, however, limited financial commitments undermine the potential for adjustment and integration. Finally, as a cost-saving device, workfare appears of dubious effectiveness unless other goals such as the reduction of dependency, labour market adjustment, reintegration or even a basic level of social assistance are set aside.

In liberal welfare states, in North America for instance, the essential policy dilemma consists in finding a balance between control and budgetary objectives. A similar dilemma exists in conservative welfare states such as Germany or France, except that budget constraints are balanced against adjustment rather than control. The prevailing logic, in this case, concerns expanding individuals' options on the labour market, not the motivations of individuals. Finally, in a social democratic welfare state such as Sweden, control reappears, because high employment levels create low caseloads, which are met by dedicated and well-funded bureaucracies, committed to facilitate adjustment and integration, even at the cost of imposing pressures on reluctant individuals.

There is no technical solution to any of these dilemmas. Choices have to be made that cannot be determined strictly by policy analysis. Values and political priorities have to prevail over cost and benefit calculus. This is even more the case in countries where two dilemmas co-exist. Canada, for instance, has to deal not only with the liberal dilemma, but also with the relevance of shifting to the conservative dilemma, which exerts a strong attraction on public actors and voters.

This conclusion brings us back to the fourth argument for workfare, which was left aside for a while: the idea of workfare as a response to voters' demands. Workfare, in whatever form, has attraction because it refers to two basic principles of liberal democracies, the idea of a minimum income for every citizen, and the idea of work as a fundamental component of citizenship. The arguments discussed above are all anchored in these two considerations, and the different approaches to social assistance and workfare all constitute attempts to respond to these concerns. The centrality of these principles helps us explain why there is a right and a left version of workfare, and why the notion has appeal at either end of the political spectrum. The tension between these principles also accounts for the impossibility of finding a simple, definitive resolution to the debate, a "one best way" that would be technically unassailable. Workfare, like many other issues in a democracy, is value-laden. Principles have to be determined before a decision can be made. This does not mean that all solutions are equal. Some measures are short-sighted, others are unfair, many are just bankrupt. In my opinion, the non-stigmatizing notions of adjustment and reintegration make more sense for a social problem and have more potential with respect to alleviating poverty and unemployment than do the individualist concepts of dependency and incentives, whose significance does not seem borne out by the facts. But even if some options seem better supported by policy analysis, the dilemmas outlined above still define a range of possibilities for the different approaches, and remind us that there are no simple, optimal responses. In the end, implementing a link between welfare and work remains a matter of democratic deliberation and political choice.[101]

1. OECD, *Labour Market Policies for the 1990s* (Paris: OECD, 1990), p. 16. A similar position was articulated in Canada by the Macdonald Commission. See Royal Commission on the Economic Union and Development Prospects for Canada, *Report*, Vol. 2 (Ottawa: Minister of Supply and Services, 1985), pp. 276, 815.

2. Björn Johnson and Bengt-Åke Lundvall, "Flexibility and Institutional Learning," in Bob Jessop, Hans Kastendiek, Klaus Nielsen and Ove K. Pedersen (eds.), *The Politics of Flexibility: Restructuring State and Industry in Britain, Germany and Scandinavia* (Aldershot: Edward Elgar, 1991), pp. 33-36.

3. OECD, *Labour Market Policies for the 1990s*, pp. 13-14, 61-63 and 83-85.

4. OECD, *The OECD Jobs Study: Facts, Analysis, Strategies* (Paris: OECD, 1994), p. 30.

5. Human Resources Development Canada, *Social Security in Canada: Background Facts* (Ottawa: HRDC, 1994), p. 44; Standing Committee on Human Resources Development of the House of Commons, *Interim Report: Concerns and Priorities Regarding the Modernization and Restructuring of Canada's Social Security System* (Ottawa: Minister of Supply and Services, 1994), p. 2.

6. OECD, *Labour Market Policies for the 1990s*, p. 88. Even in the US, this is the meaning workfare increasingly takes. Patricia M. Evans explains: "In its original and more limited sense, workfare refers to the practice of requiring unpaid work in exchange for welfare benefits. While the term is still used in this way, it also has a wider meaning that includes a variety of job-related activities that may be required as a condition of social assistance....This use of the term is increasingly common and depicts the current position in the US, where, in spite of the attention it attracts, compulsory work-for-welfare constitutes only a small component of the workfare armoury." Evans, "From Workfare to the Social Contract: Implications for Canada of Recent US Welfare Reforms," *Canadian Public Policy*, Vol. 19, no. 1 (March 1993), p. 56.

7.   Judith M. Gueron, "The Route to Welfare Reform: From Welfare to Work," *The Brookings Review*, Vol. 12, no. 3 (Summer 1994), p. 17. The same point is made in Kent Weaver, "Old Traps, New Twists: Why Welfare is so Hard to Reform in 1994," *The Brookings Review*, Vol. 12, no. 3 (Summer 1994), pp. 19-20.

8.   Quoted in Kenneth P. Ruscio, "Pork and the Public Interest," *The American Prospect*, no. 17 (Spring 1994), p. 94.

9.   James Struthers, *No Fault of Their Own: Unemployment and the Canadian Welfare State, 1914-1941* (Toronto: University of Toronto Press, 1983), p. 8. See also Michael B. Katz, "The Urban 'Underclass' as a Metaphor of Social Transformation," in M. Katz (ed.), *The Underclass Debate: Views From History* (Princeton, NJ: Princeton University Press, 1993), pp. 6-10.

10. Mary Jo Bane, "Politics and Policies of the Feminization of Poverty," in Margaret Weir, Ann Shola Orloff and Theda Skocpol (eds.), *The Politics of Social Policy in the United States* (Princeton, NJ: Princeton University Press, 1988), pp. 390-94; Andrew Armitage, "Work and Welfare: A Conceptual Review of the Relationship Between Work and Welfare," in Bill Kirwin (ed.), *Ideology, Development and Social Welfare: Canadian Perspectives*, 2nd ed. (Toronto: Canadian Scholars' Press, 1991), p. 43.

11. Charles Murray, *Losing Ground: American Social Policy, 1950-1980* (New York: Basic Books, 1984).

12. Desmond S. King, "The Establishment of Work-Welfare Programs in the United States and Britain: Politics, Ideas, and Institutions," in Sven Steinmo, Kathleen Thelen and Frank Longstreth (eds.), *Structuring Politics: Historical Institutionalism in Comparative Analysis* (Cambridge: Cambridge University Press, 1992), pp. 228-29.

13. "Welfare Reform Address by President Clinton," Kansas City, June 14, 1994.

14. "Creating Opportunity through Social Security Reform," notes for an Address by The Honourable Lloyd Axworthy, Ottawa, January 31, 1994, p. 2. Ontario's social democrat Premier Bob Rae also expressed concerns about welfare dependency. See Martin Mittelstaedt, "Sir Bob Takes on the Armada," *The Globe and Mail*, February 19, 1993, p. A1.

15. Robert Moffitt, "Incentive Effects of the US Welfare System: A

Review," *Journal of Economic Literature*, Vol. 30, no. 1 (March 1992), p. 19; Michael Charette and Ronald Meng, "The Determinants of Welfare Participation of Female Heads of Household in Canada," *Canadian Journal of Economics*, Vol. 27, no. 2 (May 1994), pp. 290-306.

16. A similar point is made by Theodore R. Marmor and Jerry L. Mashaw, in "America's Misunderstood Welfare State: Myths and Realities," *Governance*, Vol. 5, no. 4 (October 1992), p. 503.

17. Moffitt, "Incentive Effects of the US Welfare System," p. 17.

18. According to David T. Ellwood, as much as 40 percent of AFDC exits are related to earnings, as opposed to other changes such as marriage or reconciliation. These exits are often temporary, apparently because the obtained earnings are not sufficient or cannot be sustained. "Understanding Dependency," in Mary Jo Bane and David T. Ellwood (eds.), *Welfare Realities: From Rhetoric to Reform* (Cambridge, Mass.: Harvard University Press, 1994), pp. 96-98.

19. Frank S. Levy, "Work for Welfare: How Much Good Will it Do?" *American Economic Review*, Vol. 76, no. 2 (May 1986), pp. 399-404; William Julius Wilson, *The Truly Disadvantaged: The Inner City, the Underclass, and Public Policy* (Chicago: University of Chicago Press, 1987), pp. 93-106; and Lars Osberg, "Social Policy and Macro Policy in a Federal State," *Canadian Business Economics*, Vol. 2, no. 1 (Fall 1993), pp. 43-44.

20. François Vaillancourt and Julie Grignon, "L'aide sociale au Canada et au Québec 1970-1985: évolution et analyse," in *Le redressement des finances publiques québécoises: quelques pistes d'analyse* (Montréal: Institut C.D. Howe, Comité-Québec, 1986), p. 122.

21. Moffitt, "Incentive Effects of the US Welfare System," pp. 42-51; Evans, "From Workfare to the Social Contract," pp. 58-59. These studies, it must be noted, are not without problems. Benefit-cost analyses, in particular, raise difficulties. See David Greenberg and Michael Wiseman, "What Did the OBRA Demonstrations Do?", in Charles F. Manski and Irwin Garfinkel (eds.), *Evaluating Welfare and Training Programs* (Cambridge, Mass.: Harvard University Press, 1992), pp. 63-65.

22. Greenberg and Wiseman, "What Did the OBRA Demonstrations Do?"; Rebecca M. Blank, "The Employment Strategy: Public Policies

to Increase Work and Earnings," in Sheldon H. Danziger, Gary D. Sandefur and Daniel H. Weinberg (eds.), *Confronting Poverty: Prescriptions for Change* (Cambridge, Mass.: Harvard University Press, 1994), p. 186.

23. Irwin Garfinkel, Charles F. Manski and Charles Michalopoulos, "Micro Experiments and Macro Effects," in C. Manski and I. Garfinkel (eds.), *Evaluating Welfare and Training Programs*, pp. 253-73.

24. OECD, *OECD Employment Outlook* (Paris: OECD, 1993), pp. 63-64.

25. Terry R. Johnson, Daniel H. Klepinger and Fred B. Dong, "Caseload Impacts of Welfare Reform," *Contemporary Economic Policy*, Vol. 12, no. 1 (January 1994), pp. 89-101.

26. James Heckman, "Assessing Clinton's Program on Job Training, Workfare, and Education in the Workplace," National Bureau of Economic Research, Working Paper No. 4428 (Cambridge, Mass.: NBER, August 1993), p. 24.

27. Osberg, "Social Policy and Macro Policy in a Federal State," p. 44.

28. R. Walker, quoted in Evans, "From Workfare to the Social Contract," p. 63.

29. Desmond S. King and Hugh Ward, "Working for Benefits: Rational Choice and the Rise of Work-Welfare Programs," *Political Studies*, Vol. 40, no. 3 (September 1992), pp. 479-95.

30. My translation; André Bourbeau, "Aide sociale: le cas singulier du Québec," *La Presse*, December 8, 1993, p. B3.

31. An empirical refutation of Bourbeau's argument is presented in James Iain Gow, Alain Noël and Patrick Villeneuve, "Les contrôles à l'aide sociale: l'expérience québécoise des visites à domicile," *Canadian Public Policy* (forthcoming March 1995).

32. "This," write Timothy Besley and Stephen Coate, "seems consonant with the logic of the English Poor Law. By all accounts, those who ended up in the workhouse worked much harder than in a *laissez faire* equilibrium." "Workfare *versus* Welfare: Incentive Arguments for Work Requirements in Poverty-Alleviation Programs," *American Economic Review*, Vol. 82, no. 1 (March 1992), pp. 258, 260.

33. Robert Haveman and Robinson Hollister, "Direct Job Creation: Economic Evaluation and Lessons for the United States and Western Europe," in Anders Björklund, Robert Haveman, Robinson Hollister

and Bertil Holmlund (eds.), *Labour Market Policy and Unemployment Insurance* (Oxford: Oxford University Press, 1991), p. 51.

34. Stephen H. Bell and Larry L. Orr, "Is Subsidized Employment Cost Effective for Welfare Recipients? Experimental Evidence from Seven State Demonstrations," *Journal of Human Resources*, Vol. 29, no. 1 (Winter 1994), pp. 59-60.

35. Timothy Besley and Stephen Coate, "Understanding Welfare Stigma: Taxpayer Resentment and Statistical Discrimination," *Journal of Public Economics*, Vol. 48 (1992), p. 182; Wilson, *The Truly Disadvantaged*, pp. 58-61.

36. Weaver, "Old Traps, New Twists," p. 20; Marmor and Mashaw, "America's Misunderstood Welfare State," p. 504; Teresa Amott, "Reforming Welfare or Reforming the Labour Market: Lessons from the Massachusetts Employment Training Experience," *Social Justice*, Vol. 21, no. 1 (Spring 1994), pp. 35-36.

37. Wilson, *The Truly Disadvantaged*, p. 162.

38. Ailee Moon, "Should Welfare Clients Be Required to Work? Yes," in Eileen Gambrill and Robert Pruger (eds.), *Controversial Issues in Social Work* (Boston: Allyn and Bacon, 1992), p. 358.

39. Robert Pruger, "Should Welfare Clients Be Required to Work? Yes," in Gambrill and Pruger (eds.), *Controversial Issues in Social Work*, p. 374. A detailed study of public opinion indicates that in fact AFDC does not lack legitimacy. See Fay Lomax Cook and Edith J. Barrett, *Support for the American Welfare State: The Views of Congress and the Public* (New York: Columbia University Press, 1992), pp. 216-18.

40. Martin Rhodes, "The Social Dimension After Maastricht: Setting a New Agenda for the Labour Market," *International Journal of Comparative Labour Law and Industrial Relations*, Vol. 9, no. 4 (Winter 1993), p. 304.

41. Osberg, "Social Policy and Macro Policy in a Federal State," p. 43; Moffitt, "Incentive Effects of the US Welfare System," p. 13.

42. David R. Howell, "The Skills Myth," *The American Prospect*, no. 18 (Summer 1994), pp. 81-90.

43. "Even though many European countries have spent relatively more resources on labour market policy, the American evaluation industry has no counterpart on the opposite side of the Atlantic." Anders

Björklund, "Labour Market Training: The Lesson from Swedish Evaluations," in Björklund, *et al.* (eds.), *Labour Market Policy and Unemployment Insurance*, p. 86.

44. On the contrast between static and dynamic flexibility, see John Myles, "Post-Industrialism and the Service Economy," in Daniel Drache and Meric S. Gertler (eds.), *The New Era of Global Competition: State Policy and Market Power* (Montreal and Kingston: McGill-Queen's University Press, 1991), p. 364; and Danièle Leborgne and Alain Lipietz, "Two Social Strategies in the Production of New Industrial Spaces," in Georges Benko and Mick Dunford (eds.), *Industrial Change and Regional Development: The Transformation of New Industrial Spaces* (London: Belhaven Press, 1991), pp. 27-50.

45. OECD, *Labour Market Policies for the 1990s*, pp. 13-14.

46. Björn Jonzon, "Evaluation of Labour Market Policy Measures: Some Short Reflections," in Gregg M. Olsen (ed.), *Industrial Change and Labour Adjustment in Sweden and Canada* (Toronto: Garamond Press, 1988), p. 140.

47. Anders Björklund and Bertil Holmlund, "The Economics of Unemployment Insurance: The Case of Sweden," in Björklund, *et al.* (eds.), *Labour Market Policy and Unemployment Insurance*, pp. 114-15.

48. OCDE, *Perspectives de l'emploi* (Paris: OCDE, 1994), pp. 58-65; Inger Rydén, "A European Perspective: Recent Changes in Social Security in Sweden," in Elisabeth B. Reynolds (ed.), *Income Security in Canada: Changing Needs, Changing Means* (Montreal: Institute for Research on Public Policy, 1993), p. 199.

49. Björklund and Holmlund, "The Economics of Unemployment Insurance: The Case of Sweden," pp. 151, 175; OECD, *OECD Employment Outlook* (Paris: OECD, 1991), pp. 220-22.

50. "Sweden's Economy: The Nonconformist State," *The Economist*, March 7, 1987, p. 22.

51. Thomas Janoski, *The Political Economy of Unemployment: Active Labour Market Policy in West Germany and the United States* (Berkeley: University of California Press, 1990), pp. 2-3, 21-22, 26, 169-78 and 258.

52. Serge Paugam, *La société française et ses pauvres* (Paris: PUF, 1993), pp. 102-22.

53. Geoffrey Garrett and Peter Lange, "Political Response to Interdependence: What's 'Left' for the Left?", *International Organization*, Vol. 45, no. 4 (Autumn 1991), pp. 563-64; Markus M. L. Crepaz, "Corporatism in Decline? An Empirical Analysis of the Impact of Corporatism on Macroeconomic Performance and Industrial Disputes in 18 Industrialized Democracies," *Comparative Political Studies*, Vol. 25, no. 2 (July 1992), pp. 161-62.

54. Robert Boyer, "Segmentations ou solidarité, déclin ou redressement: quel modèle pour l'Europe?", in R. Boyer (ed.), *La flexibilité du travail en Europe* (Paris: La Découverte, 1986), pp. 249-64; Rebecca M. Blank and Richard B. Freeman, "Evaluating the Connection Between Social Protection and Economic Flexibility," in R. Blank (ed.), *Social Protection versus Economic Flexibility: Is There a Trade-Off?* (Chicago: University of Chicago Press, 1994), pp. 21-41.

55. Marie-Thérèse Join-Lambert, Anne Bolot-Gittler, Christine Daniel, Daniel Lenoir and Dominique Méda, *Politiques sociales* (Paris: Presses de la Fondation nationale des sciences politiques/Dalloz, 1994), pp. 506-8.

56. Bo Rothstein, "Social Justice and State Capacity," *Politics and Society*, Vol. 20, no. 1 (March 1992), p. 111.

57. OECD, *Labour Market Policies for the 1990s*, pp. 56-57.

58. Blank, "The Employment Strategy: Public Policies to Increase Work and Earnings," pp. 179-80.

59. Conseil national du bien-être social, *Réforme du bien-être social* (Ottawa: Approvisionnements et Services Canada, 1992), p. 7; Thomas J. Courchene, *Social Canada in the Millenium: Reform Imperatives and Restructuring Principles* (Toronto: C. D. Howe Institute, 1994), pp. 151-53.

60. Human Resources Development Canada, *Improving Social Security in Canada: A Discussion Paper* (Ottawa: Supply and Services Canada, 1994), pp. 45-47; Geneviève Bouchard, "Provincial Perspective: Québec," in Reynolds (ed.), *Income Security in Canada*, pp. 153-61.

61. Gordon Lafer, "The Politics of Job Training: Urban Poverty and the False Promise of JTPA," *Politics and Society*, Vol. 22, no. 3 (September 1994), pp. 370-71.

62. Maria J. Hanratty and Rebecca M. Blank, "Down and Out in North

America: Recent Trends in Poverty Rates in the United States and Canada," *Quarterly Journal of Economics*, Vol. 107, no. 1 (February 1992), p. 252.

63. Hanratty and Blank, "Down and Out in North America," p. 251; Gary Burtless, "Public Spending on the Poor: Historical Trends and Economic Limits," in Danziger, Sandefur and Weinberg (eds.), *Confronting Poverty: Prescriptions for Change*, pp. 75-83; Blank and Freeman, "Evaluating the Connection Between Social Protection and Economic Flexibility," pp. 21-41.

64. Interview with an Ontario civil servant.

65. King and Ward, "Working for Benefits," pp. 491-92.

66. Geoffrey Brennan and Loren Lomasky, *Democracy and Decision: The Pure Theory of Electoral Preferences* (Cambridge: Cambridge University Press, 1993), pp. 15-16 and 44-47. See also Jon Elster, "The Market and the Forum: Three Varieties of Political Theory," in Jon Elster and Aanund Hylland (eds.), *Foundations of Social Choice Theory* (Cambridge, Cambridge University Press, 1986), p. 111; and Jon Elster, "The Possibility of Rational Politics," *Archives européennes de sociologie*, Vol. 28, no. 1 (1987), pp. 67-103.

67. Jon Elster, *Local Justice: How Institutions Allocate Scarce Goods and Necessary Burdens* (New York: Russell Sage Foundation, 1992), pp. 238-40.

68. Cook and Barrett, *Support for the American Welfare State*, pp. 220-24.

69. Robert E. Lane, *The Market Experience* (Cambridge: Cambridge University Press, 1991), p. 335.

70. J. Donald Moon, "The Moral Basis of the Democratic Welfare State," in Amy Gutman (ed.), *Democracy and the Welfare State* (Princeton, NJ: Princeton University Press, 1988), p. 34.

71. See, for instance, Lawrence Bobo and Ryan A. Smith, "Anti-poverty Policy, Affirmative Action, and Racial Attitudes," in Danziger, Sandefur and Weinberg (eds.), *Confronting Poverty: Prescriptions for Change*, pp. 372, 394.

72. Jon Elster, "Self-Realisation in Work and Politics: The Marxist Conception of the Good Life," in Jon Elster and Karl Ove Moene (eds.), *Alternatives to Capitalism* (Cambridge: Cambridge University Press, 1989), p. 141.

73. Gøsta Esping-Andersen, *The Three Worlds of Welfare Capitalism* (Princeton, NJ: Princeton University Press, 1990).

74. Thomas Janoski, "Direct State Intervention in the Labour Market: The Explanation of Active Labour Market Policy from 1950 to 1988 in Social Democratic, Conservative, and Liberal Regimes," in Thomas Janoski and Alexander M. Hicks (eds.), *The Comparative Political Economy of the Welfare State* (Cambridge: Cambridge University Press, 1994), pp. 54-92.

75. Janoski, *The Political Economy of Unemployment*, pp. 82, 183.

76. Paugam, *La société française et ses pauvres*, p. 23.

77. See, for instance, Janoski, *The Political Economy of Unemployment*, pp. 182-90.

78. Janoski, "Direct State Intervention in the Labour Market," pp. 66-67; Günther Schmid, Bernd Reissert and Gert Bruche, *Unemployment Insurance and Active Labour Market Policy: An International Comparison of Financing Systems* (Detroit: Wayne State University Press, 1992), pp. 269-70.

79. Rothstein, "Social Justice and State Capacity," p. 111.

80. The figure's triangular representation is inspired by Swenson's work on industrial relations. See Peter Swenson, *Fair Shares: Unions, Pay, and Politics in Sweden and West Germany* (Ithaca: Cornell University Press, 1989).

81. This dilemma is identified by many authors. See, for Britain, Bill Jordan and Marcus Redley, "Polarisation, Underclass and the Welfare State," *Work, Employment and Society*, Vol. 8, no. 2 (June 1994), p. 172; for the US: Margaret Weir, Ann Shola Orloff and Theda Skocpol, "The Future of Social Policy in the United States: Political Constraints and Possibilities," in Weir, Orloff and Skocpol (eds.), *The Politics of Social Policy in the United States*, pp. 438-39; and for Canada, Armitage, "Work and Welfare," pp. 33-63.

82. Gueron, "The Route to Welfare Reform," p. 17.

83. D. Webber and G. Nass, quoted in Rianne Mahon, "From Fordism to?: New Technology, Labour Markets and Unions," *Economic and Industrial Democracy*, Vol. 8, no. 1 (February 1987), p. 38.

84. Mahon, "From Fordism to?", p. 42; Esping-Andersen, *The Three Worlds of Welfare Capitalism*, pp. 222-28.

85. See, with respect to the situation of women, Diane Sainsbury, "Dual Welfare and Sex Segregation of Access to Social Benefits: Income Maintenance Policies in the UK, the US, the Netherlands and Sweden," *Journal of Social Policy*, Vol. 22, no. 1 (January 1993), pp. 69-98.

86. Bo Rothstein, "The Crisis of the Swedish Social Democrats and the Future of the Universal Welfare State," *Governance*, Vol. 6, no. 4 (October 1993), pp. 502-05; Alan Wolfe, *Whose Keeper? Social Science and Moral Obligation* (Berkeley: University of California Press, 1989), pp. 151-84.

87. Esping-Andersen, *The Three Worlds of Welfare Capitalism*, pp. 222-28.

88. Gerard Boychuk, "Comparative Provincial Assistance Regimes: Towards a Political Economy of the Canadian Welfare States," revised version of a paper presented at the June 1994 Annual Meeting of the Canadian Political Science Association (Kingston: Department of Political Studies, Queen's University, July 1994).

89. Alain Noël, Gérard Boismenu and Lizette Jalbert, "The Political Foundations of State Regulation in Canada," in Jane Jenson, Rianne Mahon and Manfred Bienefeld (eds.), *Production, Space, Identity: Political Economy Faces the 21st Century* (Toronto: Canadian Scholars' Press, 1993), pp. 171-94.

90. Ministère de la Sécurité du revenu, *Rapport statistique mensuel. Programmes de la Sécurité du revenu, mai 1994* (Québec, Ministère de la Sécurité du revenu, 1994), p. 14.

91. Rebecca M. Blank and Maria J. Hanratty, "Responding to Need: A Comparison of Social Safety Nets in Canada and the United States," in David Card and Richard B. Freeman (eds.), *Small Differences that Matter: Labour Markets and Income Maintenance in Canada and the United States* (Chicago: University of Chicago Press, 1993), pp. 191-231.

92. Evans, "From Workfare to the Social Contract," pp. 60-63.

93. Rodney Haddow, "Canada's Experiment with Labour Market Neo-Corporatism," in Keith Banting (ed.), *Labour Market Polarization and Social Policy Reform* (Kingston: Queen's University School of Policy Studies, 1995).

94. My translation; Ministère de la Main-d'oeuvre, de la Sécurité du revenu et de la Formation professionnelle, *Partenaires pour un Québec*

compétent et compétitif: énoncé de politique sur le développement de la main-d'oeuvre (Québec, MMSRFP, 1991), p. 57.

95. Pierre Paquet, "L'évolution des politiques canadiennes et québécoises de formation des adultes depuis 1960," in Pierre Dandurand (ed.), *Enjeux actuels de la formation professionnelle* (Québec: Institut québécois de recherche sur la culture, 1993), p. 252-53.

96. John Myles and Les Teichroew, "The Politics of Dualism: Pension Policy in Canada," in John Myles and Jill Quadagno (eds.), *States, Labour Markets, and the Future of Old-Age Policy* (Philadelphia: Temple University Press, 1991), pp. 95, 99.

97. Ministère de la Main-d'oeuvre et de la Sécurité du revenu, *Rapport annuel 1982-1983* (Québec: Gouvernement du Québec, 1984), p. 7.

98. Gow, Noël and Villeneuve, "Les contrôles à l'aide sociale."

99. Gilles Lesage, "Dégraissage ou maquillage? Le remue-ménage ministériel soulève de nombreuses questions," *Le Devoir*, January 24, 1994, p. A6.

100. Mahon reaches similar conclusions through an observation of the Ontario case. Rianne Mahon, "Remise en cause des paramètres du post-fordisme au Canada et en Ontario, *Cahiers de recherche sociologique*, no. 18-19 (1992), pp. 185-215.

101. I wish to thank Stéphane Dion, James Iain Gow, Thomas Lemieux, Christopher McAll, Elisabeth Reynolds, Adil Sayeed, Jean-Philippe Thérien and three anonymous reviewers for their helpful comments on an earlier version of this paper.

P A T R I C I A   M .   E V A N S

L I N K I N G   W E L F A R E   T O   J O B S :

W O R K F A R E ,   C A N A D I A N   S T Y L E

I N T R O D U C T I O N

The federal Social Security Review launched in January 1994 is the Liberal government's highest profile policy initiative. Granted, deficit-cutting budgets are likely to make a more immediate impact on the shape of Canadian social programs. All the same, through budgets and discussion papers, the social policy field is emerging as the major arena for the battle to demonstrate that this government can indeed get Canadians back to work and reduce the deficit. A critical step toward this objective, we are told, is to transform our "passive" system of income support into an "active" one, and an important element in this process is what has come to be known as "workfare." The term originated in the United States as a contraction of "work-for-welfare," the practice of requiring recipients to provide some type of community service in exchange for benefits. However, it is now used in a much broader sense to include, as a condition of income support, the requirement that recipients participate in a wide variety of activities designed to increase their employment prospects. In effect, it translates a generalized work requirement into specific employment expectations.[1] Although the Liberal government has apparently rejected the idea of US style work-for-welfare, it is extremely interested in increasing the work-related obligations of individuals receiving income support. For reasons of jurisdiction and cost, the federal concern is primarily, but not exclusively, directed at Unemployment Insurance (UI), while provincial governments have put social assistance highest on their agendas. Replacing the provisions of the Canada Assistance Plan (CAP), which currently do not permit cost-sharing for work-for-welfare programs, with a block funding approach with few if any conditions would increase provincial interest in workfare. The implications of such intensified interest is the subject of this chapter.

The concern to make sure that people do not choose welfare over work increases when jobs are most difficult to get. This apparent paradox reflects the axiom that, when it is possible to provide more welfare, it does not seem necessary and when it is necessary, it seems impossible.[2] High levels of unemployment, along with the increasingly non-standard and tenuous nature of the jobs that do exist, are together exerting additional pressures on our income support programs. Since 1988, UI and social assistance caseloads have been on the rise, and their costs, especially in the context of concerns about the deficit, serve to direct attention to what are feared to be unsustainable demands on the social safety net. In this context, income support, once seen as a solution to the "diswelfares" of a market economy, becomes viewed as the problem.

As provincial governments struggle with the increase in social assistance costs that is exacerbated by a relatively weak economy, they encounter additional pressures. Cuts in UI further expand the demands on social assistance caseloads. The "cap on CAP" has reduced the federal share of the costs of social assistance in Ontario from 50 percent to 28 percent; British Columbia's more buoyant economy has kept the reduction there to an estimated 37 percent.[3] In their efforts to restrain social assistance spending, provinces have increased resources for caseload monitoring and fraud detection, and reduced benefits. The provinces of Quebec, Ontario, Alberta and BC have conducted well-publicized campaigns to crack down on welfare abuse, and Alberta and Quebec made cuts to benefits in 1993.[4] In June 1994, Prince Edward Island served notice to its single welfare recipients that the rent allowance portion of their social assistance benefit was to be reduced by almost 40 percent.[5] It is in this environment that increased work conditioning and workfare may appear deceptively appealing. Indeed, a recent poll indicated that

Canadians overwhelmingly (86 percent) favour "making people on welfare go to work."[6]

In contrast, I argue that workfare, in the sense of expanding the mandatory requirements for participation in work-related programs as a condition of benefit, does not belong on the current agenda, and its presence is likely to divert time and energy that could be much better spent on ensuring that employment opportunities are available for social assistance recipients. Why does workfare appear to be such an attractive option? What is the nature of the problem it is supposed to cure? What are its prospects? What do we need to do instead? In this chapter, I explore these questions through attention to four areas, beginning with an overview of current provincial practices with regard to work conditioning. There is little systematic or readily accessible information about what provinces and territories, in fact, require of employable social assistance recipients, although this information is an important starting point in the workfare debate. Secondly, several emerging trends in welfare-to-work programs are examined. In the third section I examine other types of policy initiatives that are designed to encourage the transition from welfare to work. Finally, the discussion turns to broader strategies of reform, including attention to the experience in other countries.

WORK CONDITIONING AND PROVINCIAL PRACTICES

The relationship between work and welfare, the appropriate balance between the right to receive state-financed income support and the obligation to be self-supporting, presents a continuing difficulty in social welfare in market-oriented and liberal democratic societies. Over time, the distinction between the "deserving" and the "undeserving," the principle of "less eligibility," the presence of work requirements and the stigma of receipt have all played their part in helping to ensure that benefits are not an attractive alternative to low-wage employment. At different times, the work house, the work test and work relief have provided additional buttresses to the work incentive. For example, in Toronto in 1908, at a time of high unemployment, applicants for relief were required to break up massive stones that were never used, to demonstrate their willingness to work.[7] The form of work conditioning has changed over time, although remnants of the earlier and cruder types have not completely disappeared. For example, systematically cutting off employable recipients in the spring was stopped as a widespread and accepted practice years ago; nonetheless, it continues to be done in some communities.[8]

While some Canadians may assume that social assistance is an "entitlement" in the sense of an unconditional benefit, this has never been, and is not now, the case. The CAP, which governs the conditions of federal cost-sharing for provincial social assistance, stipulates that eligibility for social assistance is to be determined solely by reference to financial need, taking into account available income and resources. It is the interpretation of "need" and "available resources" that is particularly relevant for conditions of receipt, and this interpretation appears to be changing. Individuals considered "employable" cannot voluntarily place themselves "in need" and typically must satisfy the provincial administrators that their unemployment is beyond their control and that they are making reasonable efforts to find paid work. So the CAP interpretation has always been compatible with a job search requirement and necessary acceptance by the recipient of suitable employment. However, once need is established, the CAP is interpreted to prohibit additional barriers to receipt. If a province wishes to require that recipients work in exchange for their benefits, a condition that is not related to need, these programs are not eligible for CAP dollars under the current terms of the cost-sharing agreement.[9]

The scope of activities that constitute "reasonable efforts" is expanding beyond the traditional job search and job acceptance conditions, and some provinces, for example, require participation in employment preparation programs as a condition for eligibility. This appears to be a grey area in the current interpretation of the CAP. The argument is made that this requirement is not needs-related and violates the CAP's intent. This view is lent some support by the fact that voluntary participation was made a condition of the 1985 "employability enhancement" agreements negotiated between the federal government and the individual provinces to fund a variety of employment-related initiatives for social assistance recipients. The issue of what conditions are appropriate to impose on social assistance receipt has been termed one of the most "complex and controversial" areas of welfare reform.[10]

Work requirements spell out who is expected to do what, and the consequences that may accompany the failure to fulfil the expectations. Because work-for-welfare is not permitted under the CAP, work requirements, in the Canadian context, may be thought of as falling into two conceptual categories: 1) a "work availability" requirement that typically requires recipients to accept job offers and to make efforts to find work; and 2) an "employment preparation" requirement stipulating attendance in job enhancement programs. Provincial legislation and regulations stipulate, in broad terms, the general employment expectations of social assistance recipients. In order to move beyond the formal requirements, and explore in more detail the provincial practices with respect to work requirements, I sent a questionnaire to all Deputy Ministers in the income maintenance branches of the provincial and territorial governments. Nova Scotia, Ontario and Manitoba have a "two-tiered" system, and the municipalities are primarily responsible for the administration and delivery of benefits to those considered to be employable. The information provided by Nova Scotia and Ontario reflects the general practices in these provinces. The Manitoba response reflects the practice in the municipality of Winnipeg, which accounts for about nine out of 10 employable household heads on social assistance in Manitoba.

The questionnaire requested information about what is expected of social assistance recipients: what work requirements, if any, are in place? To whom do they apply? And what penalties and sanctions may accompany any violation? It should be noted that only information about formal requirements was requested; the informal expectations, and the pressure that frequently accompanies them, is not reported. Questions were also asked about both the use of "contracts" or "action plans" for those on social assistance and the availability of "work experience" programs. All 10 provinces and the two territories responded to the questionnaire, and the findings are detailed below. Unless otherwise indicated, information is based on the completed questionnaires and follow-up discussions with some respondents.

What Is Required?

Provinces and territories were asked whether and what work-related activities were required as a continuing condition of eligibility for social assistance for employable individuals; mandatory job search and employment training were given as examples. Insisting that recipients work was only considered to be a requirement if it was also reported that a penalty could result from a failure to comply.

Three out of the 12 jurisdictions (Newfoundland, New Brunswick and the Northwest Territories) reported that no work-related conditions were imposed for the continuing receipt of social assistance. In Nova Scotia, Ontario and BC, a mandatory job search is required as is acceptance of an offer of employment. In these provinces, participation in employment programs is voluntary, but an individual who refuses to accept a place in an employment program or withdraws, without grounds, is subject once again to the mandatory job search requirement. In these circumstances, one can imagine that the requirement may well be applied with particular stringency. The situation is somewhat more ambiguous in Saskatchewan, which does not require a job search, although searches may be a component of the voluntary and agreed-upon case plan. Participation in employment and training programs is also technically voluntary, but a recipient who fails to follow through on any component of the plan, including employment training, may be subject to sanction. Questions about Saskatchewan's practice of sanctioning individuals for non-participation were raised in the House of Commons in 1991, but in response, the government reported that they found no evidence to support what was termed the "work-for-welfare" allegation.[11] In practice, other provinces may also sanction individuals on social assistance if they do not agree to participate in these programs.

In Prince Edward Island, Quebec, Manitoba and Alberta, work requirements extend beyond work availability to include an employment preparation requirement. The activities designed to increase a recipient's employability typically include employment preparation programs, educational upgrading and training, and may, in some provinces, also extend to other types of services, such as treatment for substance abuse.[12] Legislation in the Yukon is changing to require recipients, as a condition of eligibility, to take advantage of any employment or training opportunities.

The most rigorous form of sanction is the termination or suspension of benefit. This is applied, at times, in all provinces when recipients fail to fulfil their work requirement without what is deemed to be sufficient reason. Some provinces stated that sanctions would be used more frequently, were it not for poor labour market conditions, the presence of significant employment barriers among "employable" individuals and the financial hardship that cancellation imposes, particularly when dependants are involved. Because of poor local labour market conditions, proof of job search activity has been suspended in some areas. Requiring individuals to produce a regular list of contacts in areas of high unemployment is seen as not only futile and demeaning for the recipient, but also irritating to local employers. Apart from individually applied sanctions, there are occasional reports of "welfare crackdowns" when all employable recipients are informed systematically that their benefits will be cut off unless they produce proof of job search.[13]

In some provinces, employable recipients must reapply each month.[14] While this is not strictly a sanction, and so not reported by provincial administrators in the survey, it does serve as an additional monitoring mechanism. The use of time-limited benefits was also reported as a method of sanction in some provinces. In Manitoba, cheques may be issued for a shorter than usual period, pending attendance at groups or in programs. In Alberta, the length of time that a recipient is eligible for benefits depends upon his or her individual employment plan. If it is determined that a recipient can get work quickly, he or she may not be eligible for any assistance; or the support may be limited to a few days of emergency aid. The recipient may also be told that benefits will be terminated by a certain date, unless specified steps toward employment have been taken. A 1992 report expressed concern about this practice, which has at times left women and children in extremely vulnerable circumstances.[15]

Reducing benefits as a penalty for a failure to comply with work requirements was not identified as a sanction in Nova Scotia, Saskatchewan and Manitoba, but is used in other jurisdictions. Quebec applies benefit reduction as a regular and systematic penalty when a recipient refuses or abandons employment. However, because of the lack of effective monitoring mechanisms, it is used less frequently for failure to search for a job. When recipients are sanctioned, their benefits are reduced, for a period of twelve months, by $100 a month for each refusal, to a maximum of $100 a month for a household with one adult, and $200 for all others.

In summary, while there is some variation in provincial work requirements, the perception that social assistance is "unconditional" is certainly not an accurate reflection of provincial practice. While the overall relationship between provincial unemployment rates and the apparent rigour of work requirements is not consistent, the jurisdictions that do not impose work requirements (Newfoundland, New Brunswick and the Northwest Territories), are also areas of traditionally high unemployment.

Who Are the Employables?

The distinction between people able to work and those regarded as unable to work has historically been an important characteristic of social assistance programs. Originating with the Elizabethan Poor Laws of the 16th and 17th century that distinguished the "deserving" from the "undeserving," the contemporary employable/unemployable distinction helps sort out which recipients (and spouses) are subject to work requirements. Those not expected to work may receive a higher level of benefits, partly in anticipation that their need for income support is likely to last longer. However, notions of "desert" and perceptions of acceptable reasons for being in need play an important role, and employable individuals, who actually stay for longer periods on the caseload, do not generally receive automatic increases in benefits. As noted earlier, these distinctions are institutionalized in Nova Scotia, Ontario and Manitoba through a two-tier system, with the municipal level responsible for "employables" while the province directly administers the benefits for long-term "unemployable" recipients.

The growing number of employables on provincial social assistance has been a cause for concern, but any official "count" must be treated with considerable caution. The number includes some who are classified as employable but, realistically, are not; it also excludes others who would like to be employed: spouses of recipients, on-reserve Aboriginal people, many people with disabilities and, depending on the province, single mothers.[16] In addition, most changes to the definition of employability have tended to broaden it, but there is no estimation of the impact of these changes on the size of the employable caseload.[17] Changes in the qualifying conditions and length of receipt for UI will also have an effect. Despite the difficulties in estimating the numbers, higher unemployment rates can be expected to produce a higher proportion of employables on social assistance. The most recent estimate for the proportion of employables as a total of provincial caseloads in March, 1993 was 45 percent of the approximately 1.5 million social assistance cases across Canada. While this is up from 36 percent in 1981, it represents a decrease from a high of 50 percent in 1986.[18] In Metro Toronto, the depth and breadth of the recent recession are evident in an increase in the length of time employables spend on the caseload and in their changing profile. In 1988, the average length of time employables spent on the caseload was eight months; by 1993 this had increased to a year.

In addition, between 1992 and 1993, first-time applicants with some post-secondary education increased by 16.5 percent.[19]

The definition of the "employable" or "expected to work" category is not hard and fast, but reflects contemporary, prevailing socio-political values and norms about who should, and who should not, be expected to work. Most provinces exclude older people (often, in practice, those over the age of 50 or 55) and individuals with disabilities. The highest degree of contention and ambiguity about work-related expectations of individuals on social assistance centres on single mothers. These expectations have shifted significantly over time, and vary considerably from province to province.

In some provinces, single mothers with dependent children are specifically exempted from a formal work requirement. This is the case in Ontario, Nova Scotia and Manitoba. When a province does have in place a work requirement for single mothers, it may exempt some on the basis of their children's age. In BC, for example, single mothers with children under the age of 12 are now exempted from work requirements. More typically, however, provinces use school age as the formal dividing line, although the need for child care obviously extends into the after-school and weekend hours. In Quebec, single mothers with children of six years or younger are considered "temporarily unavailable" but, when their youngest child reaches school age, their benefits are reduced if they are not participating in employment-related activities. Single mothers with pre-school children are also exempted in Saskatchewan and, since 1989, in the Yukon. In PEI there is an employment "expectation" rather than a requirement for single mothers with children over the age of six, and this is reviewed on a case-by-case basis. Alberta's definition of a single mother's "availability for work" is the most stringent, and recent changes subject her to work requirements when her youngest child is six months of age, reduced from the earlier threshold of two years old.

The differences in formal requirements are likely to converge somewhat in practice. For example, the lack of a work requirement for single mothers in Nova Scotia, Ontario and Manitoba does not imply a lack of interest in their employment.[20] These provinces actively encourage employment in a variety of ways, and at times the encouragement can translate into pressure. It is equally likely that provinces that do include single mothers in their work requirements may not enforce the rules as stringently as they do for other women or men.

Single mothers on social assistance face multiple employment barriers. Like all women, they confront wage discrimination and occupational segregation in the labour market. In common with a number of social assistance recipients, they are further disadvantaged in the labour market by lower levels of education. Finally, the lack of a male parent in the household makes child care arrangements much more complicated, particularly if shift or weekend work — a frequent characteristic of women's low-wage employment — is involved. This may explain why married women with young children are more likely to be employed than single mothers.[21] According to a survey by the National Anti-Poverty Organization, 50 percent of single mothers had to leave training programs because of child care problems.[22] There is an irony in the increasing emphasis on employment for the single mother when we have abandoned a national child care strategy, and when CAP funding for child care subsidies, along with social assistance funding, is squeezed in all provinces, and capped in Ontario, Alberta and BC.

CONTRACTING WELFARE, INCREASING WORKFARE?

There is evidence across the provinces of three trends that combine to forge a closer link between jobs and welfare, and, arguably, move Canadian practice closer to workfare. They are: 1) the increasing categorization of recipients; 2) the use of work experience programs; and 3) the popularity of individualized employability plans to strengthen the work requirement. After examining these trends, I consider the usefulness of mandating participation in employment preparation programs.

First, several provinces have further refined their definitions of employability, while other provinces are considering similar changes. Instead of being simply categorized under the traditional dichotomy of employable/unemployable, individuals on the social assistance caseload may also be distinguished according to their level of participation in work-related activities.

Changes to Quebec's welfare system in 1989, for example, divided employable people into four categories and instituted variations in benefit levels on the basis of recipients' availability for and participation in employment programs. The categories, from the highest to the lowest benefits, comprise individuals who are: 1) participating in some kind of employment-related program; 2) considered temporarily unavailable for work, including those with children under school age, older people and individuals caring for those with disabilities; 3) willing and available to participate in a program, but not yet placed; and 4) new entrants to the caseload, individuals who refuse or withdraw from programs and those who have completed programs but have failed to find work. A single person without dependants, who was not participating in any program (category 4) received approximately $483 per month in January, 1992, in comparison to the basic benefit level of $597 per month for participants (category 1).[23]

Alberta's Supports for Independence program, announced in 1991, has also redefined "employability," changing the previous short-term and long-term distinction to delineate four major recipient categories based on employment expectations and circumstances: 1) "supplement to earnings" for those in employment with insufficient earnings; 2) "assured support" for those unable to work because of disability or multiple employment barriers; 3) "transitional support" for those temporarily unable to work; and 4) "employment and training support" for those participating or available to participate in employability programs. Single mothers, for example, may benefit from this change by improved access to employment programs, but the redefinition of their status has also increased their vulnerability to benefit cancellations. In addition, there are concerns that the definition of unemployability under "assured support" is more difficult to satisfy than formerly, and fewer people are receiving the somewhat higher levels of benefit available under this new category.[24]

Similar changes in Ontario were planned, but some measures have been put on hold because of budget constraints. The long-term and short-term distinction of the province's two-tiered system of social assistance was to be replaced by two programs, separating those participating in employment programs from all others on the caseload. Participants in JOBLINK, the umbrella term for a variety of employment-related programs, were to have their social assistance cheque replaced by an Employment and Training Allowance. All others would receive the Ontario Adult Benefit, with higher benefits assigned to those with disabilities, and those who could not reasonably be expected to work; the status of single mothers remained ambiguous in this proposal. While it is reasonable to provide increased benefits to cover expenses incurred because of disability or participation in employment programs, distinctions in levels of benefit that do not relate to expenses simply reflect a contemporary expression of the traditional distinction between the "deserving" and the "undeserving."

"Work experience" programs constitute the second trend apparent in the work-related programs for social assistance recipients. In many respects, these are a close "cousin" of the traditional, mandatory, work-for-welfare programs. Under the current interpretation of CAP legislation and regulations, payments made to individuals in work-for-welfare programs are not eligible for federal cost sharing, although they continue to make sporadic, and typically brief, appearances in certain provinces.[25] Work experience programs are voluntary, not mandatory, and usually, but not always, located in the public sector. While some provinces established these programs long ago, there is some evidence that their numbers are growing. New Brunswick and Metro Toronto have recently implemented new work experience programs, and the Yukon, where they have been used informally, is now considering creating a specific program. Given the possibility that the present prohibition on work-for-welfare may end with an abolition of the CAP, these programs are of particular interest.

Because they are not primarily based on the participant's obligation or duty to provide work in exchange for benefits, voluntary work experience programs may well be oriented more to benefiting the participant. In keeping with the objectives of an employability program, they also tend to be time-limited. I also distinguish work experience programs from other types of subsidized job placements in which wages are received that may be supplemented through social assistance, and under which the individual is recognized as an employee within the organization. Individuals in work experience programs continue to receive social assistance (or a re-named substitute) which is "topped up" to cover expenses and to provide a small incentive, typically in the region of $150-$250 a month. Because these top-ups, like wage-related supplements, are not related to need, they are not eligible for cost sharing under the CAP.

Conceptual distinctions among work-for-welfare, work experience programs and subsidized job placements are useful, although not so easily applied in practice when the boundaries merge between mandatory and voluntary and between earnings supplement and social assistance top-up. Work experience programs may appear particularly attractive in the current climate when the budgets of community agencies are being squeezed and social assistance caseloads are increasing. Well-designed programs can be attractive to individuals on social assistance, and they can boost confidence and improve skills; they can also have the worst characteristics of a "make work" project. But even in the best programs, issues of equity and displacement confound them. A condition of the recently inaugurated Job Incentive Project in Metro Toronto, for example, was that the job could not replace any existing employees. However, part of the impetus for the program, acknowledged by officials and agencies, is the financial squeeze on services and staff in community agencies.[26] To the extent that work experience participants replace other workers, or diminish the need to hire waged workers, they may simply provide an added push to the revolving door of low-wage employment.

The question remains whether it is legitimate to have people working side by side doing similar work who receive very different wages. In the case of families, the income from social assistance and the top-up may exceed that from minimum wage employment, but this is unlikely to be the case with single individuals. In addition, the pay scale in community agencies is usually well above the minimum wage. The Coalition for Social Assistance Reform in Ontario recommends that hours be adjusted to ensure fair wages, and that agencies be permitted to increase wages from their own budgets. A program such as Metro Toronto's has potential to provide worthwhile and beneficial opportunities. Such programs should not be dismissed out of hand, but neither can the issues of equity and displacement be ignored.

The third trend apparent in the welfare-job link is the increasing use of employability plans that represent written and agreed-upon "action plans" or "contracts." Quebec is considering ways to more effectively monitor these plans, which are likely also to emerge as a significant component in Ontario's new JOBLINK program. They are also under consideration in Manitoba. New Brunswick, which does not impose work requirements as a continuing condition of eligibility, uses written action plans for participants in their voluntary employment plans. A person who fails to follow through may be dropped from the program and, as a consequence, receive a reduced benefit. The plans are also "voluntary" in Saskatchewan, but once agreed upon, they are considered sanctionable, although sanctions would not be imposed without an opportunity for the client to discuss reasons for non-compliance. All the provinces using these agreements find them useful, citing the advantage of a clear indication of the steps needed for a person to become economically self-sufficient. The use of these plans appears to be most developed in Alberta. They have been mandatory there since the spring of 1993, and recipients are required to sign to indicate their agreement with the terms, and are informed of the consequences of not complying. Refusing to sign or unreasonably failing to comply with the terms of their agreement will result in ineligibility for benefits.

There are a number of reasons why this form of a strengthened work requirement may seem attractive. In contrast to the traditional polarization between those who emphasize the rights and entitlements of recipients and those who are concerned to increase the obligations of the poor and the general unattractiveness of receiving welfare, this new variant in the workfare approach stresses both the rights and obligations of the recipient and those of government. This is the welfare component of the wider "social contract," which calls for a redefinition of the reciprocal obligations between citizens and the state.

However appealing this type of welfare contract may appear on first consideration, there are several reasons why it should not be required as a condition of benefit. First, it defines the wrong problem. The problem is too many, not too few participants, and the issue is how to provide enough places for all the willing participants, not how to ensure that the unwilling participate. At maturity, Ontario's proposed JOBLINK will provide 100,000 places in a variety of employment-related programs. Assuming that three-quarters of the "unemployed employables" and half of the total number of single mothers might reasonably be expected to benefit from these programs, JOBLINK can only provide places to one out of every two potential participants.[27] Even the US, with its ambitious "workfare" efforts, only requires states to achieve a 20 percent participation rate among all non-exempted recipients by 1996. The challenge of employment programs is to ensure that we have enough spaces, that individuals on social assistance know about available opportunities and that voluntary participants are appropriately assessed for placement.

Second, it is often argued that mandating an employment planning process or requiring participation in employment-related activities will increase accountability for those relatively few individuals who are not seen to be making sufficient efforts to find work or improve their employment prospects. Employment assessment and planning should not be confused with a monitoring mechanism designed to sanction unwilling participants. Individuals who withdraw from the program will, of course, lose any entitlement to participation-related expenses. However, to use the planning process itself as a "test" of motivation seems wasteful of the necessary specialized resources that are required to ensure an optimal match between available programs and an individual's requirements.

Third, it is also argued that mandating the completion of an agreed-upon plan accords greater dignity, control and responsibility to the social assistance recipient by clearly spelling out rights and responsibilities. This perspective is at considerable variance with the current realities of social assistance administration, and the significant disparity of power and resources that characterize the different sides of the welfare transaction. Welfare workers typically carry very high caseloads: in some provinces, as many as 400 cases.[28] In addition, case workers frequently receive relatively little training, and the resulting climate tends to be characterized by scrutiny and stigma, not mutuality and reciprocity.

MAKING WORK PAY

Emphasizing the employment obligations of recipients, in whatever form, is only one part of the job-welfare link that characterizes Canadian income support provisions. This section contains a review of two other approaches that are also receiving considerable attention in the current efforts to move individuals from social assistance to the workforce.

Improving Incentives Through Income Support Programs

On the more positive side of the work incentive spectrum are attempts to increase the value of paid work relative to social assistance payments. Because social assistance rates, unlike wages, are based on need and geared to family size, benefits can easily exceed the earnings from low-wage work, particularly against a background of the increasingly "non-standard" nature of the employment that is available, the declining real value of the minimum wage and a rising tax burden on those with low incomes. The National Council of Welfare recently compared income from work at minimum wage with provincial social assistance rates. Not surprisingly, they found that, in most provinces, take-home earnings at the minimum wage only exceeded the amount of benefits paid in the case of single employable individuals.[29]

There have been long-standing efforts to alter the parameters of the benefit system to improve work incentives and to reduce the "tax-back rates" that social assistance recipients face when their benefits are reduced by earnings and their earnings are reduced by taxes. A recent study indicated that employed social assistance recipients in Ontario face marginal tax rates that range between 80 percent and 95 percent, and the largest component of this was the welfare tax-back.[30] Fiscal considerations and the problem of equity for the working, non-welfare poor place important constraints on the extent to which the parameters of the social assistance benefit system can be manipulated to improve work incentives. Ontario's 1989 Supports to Employment Program (STEP) significantly increased earnings exemptions and improved the tax-back rate, with particularly favourable earnings outcomes for single mothers. However, because of rising costs and the concern about the growing gap between the incomes of the welfare and non-welfare working poor, the program has been cut back.[31]

Programs operating outside the social assistance system can also help to "make work pay." Quebec, Manitoba and Saskatchewan all supplement the wages of low-income families with children. The most recent of these programs is Quebec's 1988 *Aide aux parents pour leurs revenus de travail* (APPORT), which, although primarily targeted at the working and non-welfare poor, is also open to some employed social assistance recipients. APPORT is considerably more generous than family income supplements available in Manitoba and Saskatchewan, and is also the most effective in reducing the work-welfare income differential. In 1992, the maximum benefit for a single parent with one child amounted to $2,976, and this is why Quebec was the only province in which such a parent was not financially disadvantaged by taking full-time employment at the minimum wage.[32]

The Ontario Child Income Program (OCIP) was the province's short-lived proposal to improve work incentives and reduce the programmatic separation of the working poor into welfare and non-welfare populations. Under OCIP, all low-income children were to be included in a single benefit program which replaced his or her portion of the social assistance benefit and extended income assistance to the children of the working, non-welfare poor. Because of budget constraints, it is now "on hold." However, the federal government has shown interest in this proposal. It is one of the options included in the discussion paper of the Social Security Review. In contrast, the National Council of Welfare favours a wider adoption and adaptation of APPORT, because it would be simpler to implement, and could more easily extend to the childless working poor.[33]

A third variant in the effort to increase financial incentives through income support programs are the pilot projects that the provinces of New Brunswick and BC, together with the federal government, have initiated to test the effect of time-limited income supplements on the rates of employment and earnings of social assistance recipients. The Self-Sufficiency Projects (SSPs) are directed to single parents who have been receiving social assistance for at least a year. The SSPs use an experimental model, and half of the 9,000 participants are randomly selected to receive the income supplement if they find work within a year of selection, while the others serve as a control group. They must find paid work for at least thirty hours a week; participation is voluntary, and participants selected for the income supplement can return to social assistance at any time. The supplement, which lasts for a maximum of three years, provides half of the difference between annual earnings and a benchmark, set in 1994 at $37,500 in BC and $30,600 in New Brunswick. These projects assume that the participants' experience in the low-wage labour market will pay off in terms of increased earnings when the three-year supplement period ends, and that the cost of the supplements is offset by welfare savings. The early information available suggests that it is likely to be very difficult for participants to increase their earnings to the level of the supplement over a three-year period. In February 1994, the supplement represented a sizeable proportion of the monthly earnings and approximated social assistance benefits; the average supplement paid, across both projects, was $797 per month to top up average monthly earnings of $1,912.[34] The assumptions about increased earnings and welfare savings are important to test over the long term and the projects should also provide a rich source of more general information about connections between the worlds of work and welfare. However, the outcomes are only evaluated in terms of the direct impact on participants, and cannot reveal anything about the hard-to-measure but important estimates of displacement effects.

Improving Employability

There is no question that a number of social assistance recipients are at a competitive disadvantage in the labour market because of low levels of education and skills. Programs to provide educational upgrading, employment preparation and training have been in existence for years. The rising number of "unemployed employables" on provincial social assistance caseloads provided an additional impetus to expand their participation in training, and a 1985 federal-provincial agreement diverted CAP and UI dollars to fund pilot projects, and to target participation levels in the Canadian Jobs Strategy (CJS) programs. Four years after the general agreement, separately negotiated agreements with Ottawa covered more than 3,000 approved projects. The problems that beset these training programs are also well known. Too frequently, they are not sufficiently intensive in content and/or length to meet their objectives, the skills learned are often not useful in later employment and the tendency to "cream" participants can mean that those who need them least are most likely to receive them. As a result, the evaluations of these programs generally have not been able to demonstrate the magnitude of impacts that we would like to see, and have, at times, been extremely disappointing.[35] But a recent evaluation of social assistance recipients who participated in the CJS programs reported more encouraging employment outcomes. At a two year follow-up, conducted in 1991-1992, participants spent almost double the time in employment of the comparison group (50 percent *versus* 26 percent). However, costs to government, projected over a five-year period, amounted to a $4,009 shortfall per participant because the reduction in social assistance was more than offset by increases in UI, and the costs of training exceeded the increase in tax revenues.[36] The results from the US evaluations, which use an experimental design, have indicated more success in achieving savings than in producing overall and consistent gains for participants.[37]

New Brunswick Works is an employment enhancement program that has attracted wide publicity. With an estimated price tag of $100,000 per participant, it may also be the most expensive. It begins with an individualized case plan, followed by 20 weeks of job placement. Costs then shift because the participant becomes eligible for 156 weeks of training under the UI program, which could include educational upgrading, job search skills or specialized training, skills and employment counselling and a subsidized job placement. Predictably, the New Brunswick program is receiving mixed reviews. Participants are reported as enthusiastic yet drop-out rates are high, and of course there is no guarantee of employment at the end of the road. However, as one participant put it to the New Brunswick Minister: "It's kind of like a lottery for me. I'm not sure there's a job for me at the end of it, but if you do not play, you cannot win."[38]

By international standards, Canada's overall commitment to job training is poor. An Organization for Economic Co-operation and Development (OECD) study ranked us last, out of nine OECD countries, in the preferred balance between spending on labour market programs and spending on income assistance.[39] The technological and economic changes taking place in the economy place even further pressures on training for Canada's most disadvantaged. The demand for jobs with high skill and educational qualifications is increasing with predictable effects for those who are last in the queue, and those jobs that are low-skill are increasingly temporary and part-time. This, in turn, exacerbates the ever-present tension in the allocation of training dollars between funds and programs targeted at meeting the specific requirements of the labour market, and those aimed at improving the employment prospects of the most needy.

In this section, we examined a second strategy in the Canadian effort to increase the linkage between welfare and jobs. The attempt to make work pay, unlike workfare, emphasizes the positive side of the work incentive spectrum and relies on "carrots" rather than "sticks." Improving financial incentives and enhancing employability also represent strategies that are intended to address the problem of low-wages — directly in the case of income supplements and reductions in the welfare tax-back, and indirectly through the hoped-for earnings returns on investments in training and education. In comparison to workfare, these strategies offer a more constructive approach to the employment problems facing individuals on social assistance. Their effectiveness, however, will be severely blunted if unemployment remains high.

WORK AND WELFARE: SWEDEN AND THE UNITED STATES

All the efforts to make people work, and to make work pay, will have little effect if there are no jobs available. It is increasingly suggested that countries can generate employment by pursuing greater labour market "flexibility," which translates into lowering social protection, reducing the size of the public sector, lowering the minimum wage and encouraging the growth of low-wage employment.[40] This strategy is thought to lower unemployment rates, along with wage rates, but it also increases inequality. In contrast, others emphasize the importance of maintaining a high-wage strategy and underline the positive role that national employment strategies and income support programs can play in support of this objective.[41] The US and Sweden are often cited as illustrations of these opposing strategies, with the former more concerned with the welfare side of the equation and the latter focussed on good employment. In the context of concern to transform our "passive" programs, it is useful to review briefly the policy emphases in these two countries.

Sweden is well known for its active labour market policies, which are described as "institutional" rather than "marginal" because of the attention given to preventing unemployment, as opposed to simply alleviating its consequences.[42] These policies have included an expansion of public sector employment, the creation of counter-cyclical temporary jobs, extensive labour market training and mobility grants, all of which are bolstered by its "solidaristic" tripartite wage policies. Until recently, these policies helped to keep unemployment at comparatively low rates. Now on the verge of European Union membership and anxious to reduce its inflation and taxes, Sweden finds itself much less sheltered from the general economic and political pressures that are now affecting its social programs.

Unemployment in Sweden is now eight percent, excluding those in government public service work or training programs.[43] Despite these pressures, and cutbacks in their social programs that appear minimal in the Canadian context, Sweden's emphasis on public sector employment and active labour market policies continues, and voters there recently returned the Social Democrats to power, after a three-year period of rule by a centre-right coalition. The work-oriented nature of the Swedish system also permeates social security. Unemployed individuals eligible for benefits and employable social assistance recipients must register with the local office of the national employment service, where, by law, information on all job vacancies must be sent. They must also engage in job search and accept employment even if it requires relocation, but income assistance cannot be denied for refusal to engage in training or rehabilitation.[44] However, there is little apparent concern to provide extra incentives for individuals to take up training opportunities. Unemployment benefits are typically higher than training allowances, although an individual who begins training while on unemployment will not have his or her benefits reduced. In a country with a tradition of active employment measures, generally high-quality training and temporary public service jobs leading to "mainstream" and well-paid jobs, the call for "workfare," in the North American sense of increasing the work-conditioning of benefits, appears to have little resonance.[45]

The US tradition is quite different and its active policy measures have focussed much more on the issue of welfare and dependency than good jobs. Although unemployment is at its lowest in four years (5.9 percent), the poverty rates are the highest since 1965, with the exception of one year during the Reagan administration.[46] The concern about welfare has been directed almost entirely to single mothers, in part because state aid to employable single adults is minimal, and at times, non-existent, and aid to families with an unemployed father has only recently become a mandated program. Every President since Lyndon Johnson has attempted to reform welfare, and an important lesson from their experience is that, in the absence of strategies to address the problems of the low-wage labour market, attempts to marry the objectives of fiscal restraint, the alleviation of poverty and increased work incentives present intractable dilemmas. As a US policy analyst noted more than 20 years ago, this is the context in which more coercive, but not more effective, welfare policies develop.[47]

Following a long history of changes to strengthen the work requirements in the US Aid to Families with Dependent Children (AFDC) program, the Family Support Act of 1988, steeped in the language of contract and mutual responsibilities, was introduced. The legislation attracted a wide consensus by providing "carrots" in the form of increasing employment-related initiatives, and "sticks" by further tightening work requirements that obliged states to mandate participation in the Job Opportunity and Basic Skills (JOBS) program for single mothers with children over three years old. While some of the results from California's program, which emphasized education, look promising, even enthusiasts are sceptical of the prospects of continued achievement. State governments across the country have been at times unable, and at times unwilling to take full advantage of the federal funds available for program development; in 1991 this meant that only about 10 percent to 15 percent of recipients were participating.[48]

The latest proposal is President Clinton's announcement in June 1994 to "end welfare as we know it" by limiting AFDC receipt to two years of benefits; if a recipient is unable to find a job in the private sector, minimum wage public sector employment may be available. It remains to be seen how these proposals will be fleshed out in specifics and how the issue of cost will be dealt with. Given that the reforms are targeted exclusively at young single mothers (excepting those who have children younger than a year), there may be considerable and costly barriers to employment in the form of child care needs. Over the past two decades, the value of AFDC benefits has declined by 25 percent, taking into account the value of food stamps. In addition, the increasing use of sanctions and penalties that extend well beyond employment-related behaviour is graphically underlined in the following comment:

> Wisconsin's "learnfare" reduces the checks of welfare mothers whose children are truant; Maryland's "healthfare" docks mothers when their children do not receive health check-ups or immunizations; New Jersey's "wedfare" offers a bonus to women who marry, while its "family cap" lowers the grant to women who have an additional child while on the rolls. And some politicians talk about making Norplant, the contraceptive implant, a condition for receiving AFDC money.[49]

CONCLUSION

As Canada continues to grapple with deficit reduction and social program reform, the issue of "workfare" will remain firmly on the agenda. Workfare, in the sense of increasing the obligations of social assistance recipients to take up education, training or community service as a condition of their entitlement resonates in a political and economic environment that has identified social programs, rather than unemployment, as a major culprit in increasing both individual "dependency" and the deficit. However, this review of the practices, trends and issues related to workfare suggests that "making people work" is not the direction in which we should be channelling our limited resources. While it is a challenge to ensure the availability of good quality employment programs, the greater challenge is to ensure that there are jobs in which to invest the newly acquired skills. Enforcing a welfare "contract" by requiring participation in employment-related programs as a condition of social assistance for employable individuals or penalizing them for non-participation does not help to meet these challenges, and entails administrative and monitoring costs we can ill afford. Efforts to "make work pay," directly through income supplements and indirectly through programs designed to increase individual employability, offer more constructive definitions of the welfare "problem" and the accompanying solution, but their potential impact will be limited during times of high unemployment.

The contrasting examples of Sweden and the US suggest that workfare can only be understood in context. What makes "workfare" work or, more accurately in the Swedish case, what makes it largely irrelevant, is the country's commitment to active, not passive, labour market and employment policies. US workfare, like its welfare system, seems inexorably driven to become leaner and meaner, relying increasingly on regulations and sanctions in the welfare system and deregulation in the labour market.

In Canada, the flavour of the workfare debate is similar to that which surrounded the US Family Support Act in 1988. The language of reciprocal obligations is attracting attention, but it offers little substance. Social programs do need reform, but increasing the work obligations of social assistance recipients is not part of the solution, and only likely to deflect us further from the more important task of tackling the jobs deficit with an active employment strategy that confronts our continuing high level of unemployment in ways that move us beyond training and education to tackle the availability of jobs at decent wages.[50] Increasing the work-related obligations of social assistance recipients may appear relatively innocuous when unemployment is low. However, when workfare is viewed as part of the solution to the fiscal strains imposed by high unemployment, it is likely to prove punitive, costly and ineffective.[51]

NOTES

1. For discussion, see Michael Wiseman, "Workfare and Welfare Reform,"
   in H. Rodgers (ed.), *Beyond Welfare: New Approaches to Problems of Poverty
   in America* (London: M.E. Sharpe, 1988), pp. 14-38. See also Richard
   Nathan, *Turning Promises into Performance: The Management Challenge of
   Implementing Workfare* (New York: Columbia University Press, 1993),
   p. 14. He attributes the first use of the term to Richard Nixon in
   1969, and suggests that it was not until several years later that the
   media adapted it as a contraction for work-for-welfare.
2. David Macarov, *Work and Welfare: The Unholy Alliance* (Beverly Hills:
   Sage, 1980), p. 24.
3. Because of the relatively low level of increases in Alberta's CAP expenditures, the federal contribution has only been reduced to 47 percent.
   Paul A. R. Hobson and France St-Hilaire, "Fiscal Transfers and the
   Federal Role in Income Security," in Elisabeth B. Reynolds (ed.),
   Income Security in Canada: Changing Needs, Changing Means (Montreal:
   Institute for Research on Public Policy, 1993), p. 135.
4. National Council of Welfare, *Welfare Incomes 1993* (Ottawa: NCW,
   1994), p. 12.
5. François Dumaine, "Is the new economy allergic to fairness?", *The
   Globe and Mail*, August 11, 1994.
6. "86 percent Favour Making Welfare Recipients Go To Work,"
   Publication release, Gallup Canada, March 31, 1994.
7. Michael J. Piva, *The Condition of the Working Class in Toronto:
   1900-1921* (Ottawa: University of Ottawa Press, 1979), p. 74.
8. Ontario, *Transitions: Report of the Social Assistance Review Committee*, prepared for the Ministry of Community and Social Services (Toronto:
   Queen's Printer, 1988), p. 227; see also Barbara Blouin, "Below the
   Bottom Line: The Unemployed and Welfare in Nova Scotia,"
   Canadian Review of Social Policy, nos. 29 and 30, (Summer, Winter
   1992), pp. 112-31.
9. Ernie S. Lightman, "Conditionality and Social Assistance: Market
   Values and the Work Ethic," in Graham Riches and Gordon

Ternowetsky (eds.), *Unemployment and Welfare* (Toronto: Garamond Press, 1990), p. 94.

10. Ontario, *Transitions*, p. 226.

11. See discussion in National Council of Welfare, *Welfare Reform* (Ottawa: NCW, 1992), p. 33; and House of Commons, *Debates*, March 22, 1991, p. 18879.

12. For example, the Prince Edward Island regulations (5.a) state that an individual receiving assistance is required, as a condition of continuing eligibility "[t]o accept employment where reasonable opportunities arise, or to undergo training or treatment or both necessary to improve or restore his capacity to support himself and his dependants."

13. See, for example, Craig McInnes, "49,000 on welfare in BC told benefits will be cut if they do not seek work," *The Globe and Mail*, August 5, 1989.

14. National Council of Welfare, *Welfare Reform*, p. 10.

15. Guyn Cooper Research Associates, *Supports for Independence and its Effect on Women* (Calgary: Alberta Advisory Council on Women's Issues, April 1992), pp. 35-36.

16. The term single mother is used because the overwhelming number of single parents on social assistance are female. In 1988, the female proportion of single parents claiming assistance in Quebec was 95 percent; calculated from table 4.9a, in Health and Welfare Canada, *Inventory of Income Security Programs in Canada: July 1990* (Ottawa: Minister of Health and Welfare, 1992), p. 84. A similar proportion is reported for Manitoba: see Manitoba Advisory Council on the Status of Women, *Single-Parent Families Report* (Winnipeg: MACSW, 1990), p. 17. For an earlier discussion on work requirements for single mothers, see Patricia M. Evans and Eilene McIntyre, "Welfare, Work Incentives and the Single Mother: An Interprovincial Comparison," in J. Ismael (ed.), *Canadian Welfare State: Evolution and Transition* (Edmonton: University of Alberta Press, 1987), pp. 101-25.

17. Canadian Labour Market and Productivity Centre (CLMPC), "Task Force Report on Social Assistance Recipients," in *Report of the CLMPC's Task Forces on the Labour Force Development Strategy* (Ottawa: CLMPC, 1990), p. 130.

18. For the 1993 estimate, see Human Resources Development Canada, *Improving Social Security in Canada: A Discussion Paper* (October 1994),

p. 20; earlier estimates are from CLMPC, "Task Force Report on Social Assistance Recipients," p. 136. It is not clear why the proportion of employable individuals on the caseload was higher in 1986 than in 1993. It may reflect a combination of factors including increases in the number of single mothers, a loosening of disability determination, greater scrutiny of employable applicants and a decline in refugees, who are not eligible to work until their status is determined.

19. Jane Coutts, "Welfare profile moves upscale," *The Globe and Mail*, November 23, 1993.

20. For discussion of Ontario and Nova Scotia's efforts to increase employment among single mothers on social assistance, see Patricia M. Evans, "Work Incentives and the Single Mother: Dilemmas of Reform," *Canadian Public Policy*, Vol. 14, no. 2 (June 1988), pp. 125-36; and Stella Lord, "Social Assistance and 'Employability' for Single Mothers in Nova Scotia," in A. Johnson, S. McBride and P. Smith (eds.), *Continuities and Discontinuities: The Political Economy of Social Welfare and Labour Market Policy in Canada* (Toronto: University of Toronto Press, 1994), pp. 191-206.

21. Martin D. Dooley, "Recent Changes in the Economic Welfare of Lone Mother Families in Canada: The Roles of Market Work, Earnings and Transfers," in Joe Hudson and Burt Galaway (eds.), *Single Parent Families: Perspectives on Research and Policy* (Toronto: Thompson Educational Publishing, 1993), pp. 120-23.

22. Cited in CLMPC, "Task Force Report on Social Assistance Recipients" (1990), p. 141.

23. National Council of Welfare, *Welfare Reform*, pp. 17-18.

24. Guyn Cooper Research Associates, *Supports for Independence and its Effect on Women*, pp. 35-36.

25. See, for examples and discussion, Leslie Bella, "Work for Welfare: Alberta's Experiment in New Improved Work-For-Relief," *Perception*, Vol. 7, no. 1 (September-October 1983), pp. 14-16; Melanie Hess, "Traditional Workfare: Pros and Cons," prepared for the Ontario Social Assistance Review Committee, Research Document 21, (April 1987); and Ernie S. Lightman, "Work Incentives Across Canada," *Journal of Canadian Studies*, Vol. 26, no. 1 (Spring 1991), pp. 120-38.

26. See "Training Proposal" Metropolitan Toronto Job Incentive Project,

December 14, 1993; and Jane Coutts, "Job training for welfare clients proposed," *The Globe and Mail*, March 9, 1993.

27. These estimates are based upon figures in National Council of Welfare, *Who Are the People on Welfare?* (Ottawa: NCW, 1994), table 1, p. 1 and graph C, p. 8.

28. Clayton Ruby, "The Devastation Behind Metro Council's Frugality," *The Toronto Star*, June 1, 1994.

29. National Council of Welfare, *Incentives and Disincentives to Work* (Ottawa: NCW, 1993), table 11, p. 34. This comparison excludes the incentives to the two-earner couple working full-time at the minimum wage, who would not be eligible for social assistance.

30. Ken Battle and Sherri Torjman, *The Welfare Wall: The Interaction of the Welfare and Tax Systems* (Ottawa: Caledon Institute, 1993), p. 21.

31. Changes to STEP in 1992 made recipients ineligible during the first three months they are on the caseload and lowered the level of eligible earnings by excluding STEP exemptions in the process of determining financial eligibility.

32. National Council of Welfare, *Incentives and Disincentives to Work*, table 11, p. 34.

33. National Council of Welfare, *Income Assistance for Families with Children*, Social Security Backgrounder No. 3 (Ottawa: NCW, 1994), pp. 7-8.

34. Social Research and Demonstration Corporation, "The Self-Sufficiency Project Program Fact Sheet" (January 1994), table 4.

35. See, for example, CLMPC, "Task Force Report on Social Assistance Recipients," pp. 139-42; and Errol Porter, "The Long-Term Effects of Three Employment Programs for Social Assistance Recipients" (Toronto: Ministry of Community and Social Services, Research and Program Evaluation Branch, November 1991).

36. Human Resources Development Canada, *Evaluation of Employability Initiatives for Social Assistance Recipients (SARS) in CJS* (Ottawa: HRDC, Program Evaluation Branch, April 1994).

37. Judith M. Gueron, "Welfare Reform in the United States: Strategies to Increase Work and Reduce Poverty," in Elisabeth B. Reynolds (ed.), *Income Security in Canada: Changing Needs, Changing Means* (Montreal: Institute of Research on Public Policy, 1993), pp. 171-81; and Evans,

"Work Incentives and the Single Mother," pp. 58-61.

38. Kevin Cox, "N.B. bragging angers welfare recipients," *The Globe and Mail*, February 12, 1994. See also, Geoffrey York, "Ottawa starts reweaving safety net," *The Globe and Mail*, December 17, 1993; and John DeMont, "Fast Frank: How New Brunswick's premier turned his province into Canada's social laboratory," *Maclean's*, Vol. 107, no. 15, April 11, 1994, pp. 22-28.

39. Michel Demers, "Responding to the Challenges of the Global Economy: The Competiveness Agenda," in Frances Abele (ed.), *How Ottawa Spends: The Politics of Competitiveness, 1992-1993* (Ottawa: Carleton University Press, 1992), table 6.2, p. 161.

40. Organization for Economic Co-operation and Development (OECD), "Employment/Unemployment Study," Draft Policy Report, General Secretariat (January 1994); and newspaper coverage of the final report: Peter Cook, "OECD jobs plan a menu of solutions," *The Globe and Mail*, June 6, 1994, p. B1; and Terence Corcoran, "OECD report no cause for fuss," *The Globe and Mail*, June 8, 1994.

41. See, for example, essays in Daniel Drache (ed.), *Getting on Track: Social Democratic Strategies for Ontario* (Montreal: McGill-Queen's University Press, 1992); and Armine Yalnizyan, *Defining Social Security, Defining Ourselves* (Toronto: Canadian Centre for Policy Alternatives/Social Planning Council of Metropolitan Toronto, May 1993).

42. For a good discussion of the development of the Swedish welfare state, see Gøsta Esping-Andersen and Walter Korpi, "From Poor Relief to Institutional Welfare States: The Development of Scandinavian Social Policy," in R. Erickson, E. Hansen, S. Ringen and H. Uusitalo (eds.), *The Scandinavian Model: Welfare States and Welfare Research* (London: M.E. Sharpe, 1987), pp. 39-74. For discussion of pressures, see B. Gustafsson and N. Klevmarken, "Taxes and Transfers in Sweden: Incentive Effects on Labour Supply," in A. Atkinson and G. Mogensen (eds.), *Welfare and Work Incentives* (Oxford: Claredon Press, 1993), pp. 50-133; and S. Marklund, "The Decomposition of Social Policy in Sweden," *Scandinavian Journal of Social Welfare*, Vol. 1 (1992), pp. 2-11.

43. Jean-Michel Normand, "Sweden keeps jobless feeling useful," *Guardian Weekly*, May 1, 1994, p. 14.

44. The Swedish Supreme Administrative Court has ruled that assistance cannot be denied for refusal to engage in training or rehabilitation. Information from Joakim Palme, Swedish Institute for Social Research. For information on other requirements, see Gustafsson and Klevmarken, "Taxes and Transfers in Sweden," pp. 118-21.

45. Despite the generous levels of unemployment compensation, Swedish concerns about the disincentive effects of transfer programs focus primarily on early retirement and sickness provisions. See Inger Rydén, "A European Perspective: Recent Changes in Social Security in Sweden," in Reynolds (ed.), *Income Security in Canada*, p. 194; and Marklund, "Decomposition of Social Policy in Sweden."

46. Martin Walker, "Why ABC may spell defeat for Democrats," *Guardian Weekly*, October 16, 1994.

47. Martin Rein, "Work Incentives and Welfare Reform in Britain and the United States," in B. Stein and S. Miller (eds.), *Incentives and Planning in Social Policy* (Chicago: Aldine Publishing, 1973), p. 167.

48. Mark Greenberg, *The Devil is in the Details: Key Questions in the Effort to "End Welfare as We Know It"* (Washington, DC: Center for Law and Social Policy, 1993), p. 4. For further discussion, see Patricia M. Evans, "From Workfare to the Social Contract: Implications for Canada of Recent US Welfare Reforms," *Canadian Public Policy*, Vol. 19, no. 1 (March 1993), pp. 54-67.

49. Mimi Abramovitz and Frances Fox Piven, "Scapegoating Women on Welfare," *New York Times*, September 2, 1993.

50. We cannot deal adequately here with the multiple strategies needed to create and bolster good employment, an issue that is disappearing as rapidly from the political agenda as concerns about the deficit and international competitiveness increase. For alternative views on redirecting social and economic policies to support good jobs, see essays in Drache (ed.), *Getting on Track*; Yalnizyan, *Defining Social Security*; and The Ecumenical Coalition for Economic Justice, *Reweaving Canada's Social Programs: From Shredded Safety Net to Social Solidarity* (Toronto: ECEJ, 1993).

51. I would like to thank the 12 provincial and territorial officials for their help and co-operation in responding to my questionnaire and, in many cases, answering a number of follow-up questions. Thanks are also due

to Gilles Séguin, John Stapleton and two anonymous reviewers for their careful and thoughtful comments on an earlier draft; remaining weaknesses are, unfortunately, the sole responsibility of the author.

E L I S A B E T H   B .   R E Y N O L D S

SUBSIDIZED EMPLOYMENT PROGRAMS

AND WELFARE REFORM:

THE QUEBEC EXPERIENCE

INTRODUCTION

This chapter is an attempt to assess the effectiveness of a subsidized employment program established in Quebec aimed at moving welfare recipients off the rolls and into the labour force. It is hoped that the conclusions drawn from this exercise will help inform the debate over future reforms in the area of welfare-to-work transition.

Since the late 1960s and early 1970s, both American and Canadian governments, as well as those of a number of European countries, have experimented with direct job creation programs, and new pilot projects have been put in place in recent years.[1] Faced in the 1970s with high rates of unemployment, these governments funded a number of projects that provided jobs in the public sector or offered wage or hiring subsidies to employers in the private sector. Today, governments again face high unemployment rates, with the added dimension of a trend toward greater long-term unemployment, and thus are trying to tinker with previous models used to create the right balance of incentives without provoking abuse.

The goal of such experiments has been in general to increase the employment rate in certain economically depressed regions, or to assist certain groups in society who face the greatest barriers to employment — e.g., the long-term unemployed, welfare recipients, youth, coal miners, Aboriginal people, the handicapped *etc*. In addition, such programs have been seen as tools for investing in the human capital of participants, by imparting skills and work experience to increase their employment opportunities in the future.

Such programs have been controversial, and have been criticized on many fronts. Critics variously claim that the programs provide cheap labour to employers, creating an incentive for employers to "churn" workers through the firm; that they create "deadweight costs" (i.e., they subsidize workers who would have been employed anyway or fill jobs that would have been filled even without a subsidy); and that they create substitution effects, whereby subsidized jobs come at the expense of other employees' jobs. In their favour, these programs have been credited with helping disadvantaged workers enter the labour force, creating jobs in regions with high unemployment, preventing the negative effects of long-term unemployment and, in general, promoting greater income equality and redistribution.

Many of these programs have been part of a larger effort to reform government income support policies. Most member countries of the Organization for Economic Co-operation and Development have reoriented income security from being a "passive" cash transfer to being a more "active" policy involving employment enhancement programs. Concern over the development of a welfare-dependent population as well as a greater understanding of the negative consequences of long-term unemployment and poverty in general have led to policies that allow or oblige welfare recipients to enhance their employability through further education, training or work experience, or a combination of these.[2]

While such measures have existed since the late 1960s, evaluations of the various programs did not begin in earnest until the mid-1970s in the United States, and it is only since the mid-1980s that evaluation results have been considered fairly robust.[3] Since that time, a number of subsidized employment programs across the US have been evaluated to determine their success at integrating disadvantaged workers into the labour force, increasing earnings and reducing welfare costs. In Canada, rigorous evaluation processes (one of the goals of the Four Corners Agreement[4]) have not been developed until recently. Experiments or pilot projects have been initiated in a number of provinces, either with federal co-operation or by the provinces on their own. (Responsibility for welfare falls under provincial jurisdiction. However, funding is shared with the federal government.)

It is too early to analyze the results of most experiments across the country. In Quebec, results showing the effects over a 19-month period of the province's subsidized work program, *Programme d'aide à l'intégration en emploi* (PAIE), have recently been released.

The first part of this chapter constitutes a brief review of recent welfare reforms in Quebec and provides profiles of the welfare population. We then look specifically at the Quebec subsidized wage program, PAIE.

WELFARE REFORM IN QUEBEC

Welfare reform in Quebec over the past three decades has exhibited many of the broad trends identified in welfare state theory and practice in North America over the period. Beginning as aid to the disabled, the blind and needy mothers, access to welfare, or social assistance, became a right for any needy individual in the late 1960s, first provincially, following the findings of Quebec's Boucher Commission, and nationally with the introduction of the Canada Assistance Plan in 1966. Over the subsequent two decades, numerous programs were introduced that were focussed on creating work incentives for those on social assistance, including wage supplements, training programs and further education.

Historically, Quebec has had the second highest rate of dependence (number of welfare recipients including children divided by the active population aged 15-64) in the country, following the Atlantic provinces. In comparison to Ontario, the most similar province to Quebec in terms of size, labour market and industrial base, Quebec has had a consistently higher rate of dependence for most of the past 20 years (see table 1). Part of this can be attributed to Ontario's more productive economy — its larger GDP per capita and significantly lower rates of unemployment. The GDP per person between 1981 and 1991 was on average 22 percent higher in Ontario ($21,446) than in Quebec ($17,502).[5]

The 1980s were a relatively volatile time with regard to Quebec's welfare rolls. The province was hit particularly hard by the 1981-82 recession and experienced the highest rate of dependency in all of Canada from 1981 to 1987.[6] Beginning in 1987, welfare rolls in Quebec began to decline. The rate of dependence fell from 20 percent to 16.4 percent

Figure 1

Evolution of the Number of Welfare Recipients in Quebec and Ontario, 1975-1993

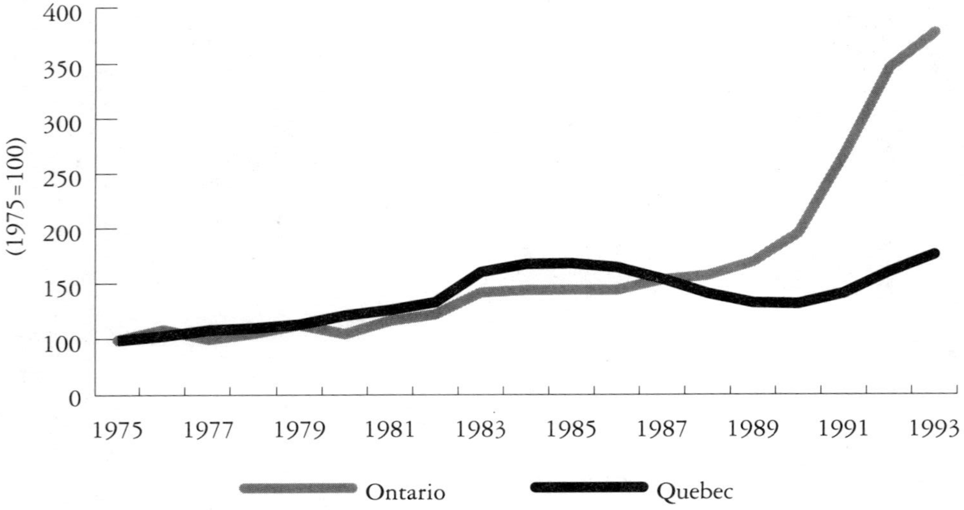

Table 1

Comparison Between Quebec and Ontario: Welfare Rolls, Rate of Dependence and Unemployment Rate, 1975-1993

	Quebec			Ontario			
Years	Number	Rate of	Rate of	Unemployment	Number	Rate of	Rate of	Unemployment

1976	435 231	3.8%	16.2%	8.7%	367 943	9.4%	9.5%	6.2%
1977	457 170	5.0%	16.6%	10.3%	338 909	-7.9%	8.5%	7.0%
1978	464 666	1.6%	16.4%	10.9%	356 324	5.1%	8.6%	7.2%
1979	477 982	2.9%	16.5%	9.6%	382 224	7.3%	9.0%	6.5%
1980	512 068	7.1%	17.1%	9.8%	354 798	-7.2%	8.2%	6.8%
1981	533 080	4.1%	17.6%	10.3%	394 593	11.2%	8.8%	6.6%
1982	561 999	5.4%	18.3%	13.8%	413 783	4.9%	9.2%	9.7%
1983	676 124	20.3%	22.3%	13.9%	480 320	16.1%	10.5%	10.3%
1984	706 204	4.4%	22.9%	12.8%	487 265	1.4%	10.5%	9.0%
1985	708 863	0.4%	22.6%	11.8%	487 898	0.1%	10.3%	8.0%
1986	693 874	-2.1%	21.9%	11.0%	487 339	-0.1%	10.0%	7.0%
1987	649 556	-6.4%	20.0%	10.3%	518 864	6.5%	10.4%	6.1%
1988	594 016	-8.6%	17.9%	9.4%	531 558	2.4%	10.4%	5.0%
1989	559 299	-5.8%	16.7%	9.3%	572 860	7.8%	11.0%	5.1%
1990	555 907	-0.6%	16.4%	10.1%	659 285	15.1%	12.5%	6.3%
1991	594 879	7.0%	17.5%	11.9%	898 184	36.2%	17.0%	9.6%
1992	674 874	13.4%	19.9%	12.8%	1 163 712	29.6%	22.0%	10.8%
1993	741 397	9.9%	21.8%	13.1%	1 272 429	9.3%	23.7%	10.6%

Source: Ministère de la Sécurité du revenu du Québec. "De l'aide sociale à la sécurité du revenu. Rapport statistique 1992-93." janvier 1994.

¹The formula used is the Number of Clients over the Active Population (15-64) as recorded by Statistics Canada Cat. 71-201 (1993), p. 35 for Quebec and p. 38 for Ontario.

in 1990, as the economy recovered and the government introduced more restrictive reforms.[7] In Ontario, by contrast, welfare rolls began to increase in 1987. In 1989, for the first time in history, the absolute number of welfare recipients in Ontario surpassed the number in Quebec. By 1993, Ontario's rate of dependence had reached 23.7 percent, an all-time provincial high, and higher than the rate for Quebec. During this period, Ontario increased benefits and widened the eligibility criteria for welfare. From 1986 to 1990, benefits for single parents and a couple with two children on welfare increased in real terms by 21 and 27 percent respectively in Ontario, compared to a decline in benefits of one and eight percent for the equivalent households in Quebec.[8]

In reaction to the sharp increase in the number of welfare recipients in Quebec from 1977 to 1987 (44 percent), Quebec reassessed its welfare policies. As in many other states and provinces in North America, its welfare population had changed over the previous decade. In Quebec, the changes were manifested in four significant ways:

- the number of single adults on welfare doubled over this time period;
- the average age of the recipients dropped from 36 to 32 from 1971 to 1987;
- those who were considered employable represented a much greater proportion of recipients — from 33 percent of adults in 1971 to 73 percent in 1987; and
- the number of families on welfare increased by 57 percent over the same time period, due largely to an increase in the number of single-parent families.

It should be noted that part of the significant growth in the number of employable people on welfare may have to do with definitions. For example, in the early 1970s, mothers with children under the age of six were not considered employable; this is no longer the case.

These changes corresponded with social and economic changes taking place at the macro and micro level: international trade liberalization leading to greater global competition, a restructuring of the Canadian economy and changes in the Canadian family. The restructuring itself began with the recession of 1981-82, and continued through the recession of 1990-92, when many sectors of the Canadian economy, primarily manufacturing, experienced a significant decline in output. One of the outcomes of this process has been what appears to be a permanent shedding of jobs, more seriously in the 1990-92 recession than in 1981-82.[9] Throughout this process, there has been an increasing demand for higher skilled workers, and this has reduced opportunities for less educated workers. With the "natural" rate of unemployment estimated to be between six and eight percent,[10] and an increase in the number of part-time jobs, the unemployed have a tougher time finding full-time work over the long-term.[11] In addition, the Bank of Canada's current low inflation objective has kept real interest rates high, tightening credit for investment and consumption, thus slowing the recovery and job creation.

One of the major consequences of these changes has been an increase in the number of long-term unemployed (those without jobs for more than a year). In Quebec in 1976, 3.9 percent of those unemployed were considered long-term unemployed. In 1987, that proportion had more than tripled to 13.5 percent.[12] Long-term unemployment is a particular problem in that it leads to:

- a decrease in future productivity as the long-term unemployed do not maintain skill levels; and
- a more general loss in human capital, as the long-term unemployed suffer greater depression and are more likely to indulge in substance abuse and violent behaviour,[13] leading to greater costs for society.

It is against this backdrop that Quebec introduced its welfare reforms in 1989.

The Two-Tier Welfare System

The objectives of the Quebec welfare reforms of 1989 were three-fold: first, to identify those on welfare who could be considered employable; second, to introduce a stricter and more all-encompassing system of work incentives; and third, to compile better statistics on the welfare population in order to better understand the dynamics of welfare use. Welfare recipients are divided into two large groups: those who are between the ages of 18 and 64 and are considered employable are part of *Actions positives pour le travail et l'emploi* (APTE), while those who are not considered employable (i.e., the disabled, or those who are unable to work due to physical or mental illness) are eligible for *Soutien financier* (SF).

Since 1991, the percentage of households on APTE *versus* those on SF has remained relatively constant, with 78 percent of households on APTE, and 20 percent on FS, as of March 1994. The remaining two percent are under state care for other reasons. Of a total of 741,387 individuals on welfare in March 1993,[14] 56 percent were considered employable, 13 percent were considered unemployable and the remaining 30 percent were children.

The 56 percent (or 415,837) of the welfare population considered employable are then divided into four different categories, according to their ability and desire to participate in employment enhancement programs. Benefit levels rise or fall according to the category into which the recipient falls.

The rest of this chapter is focussed on the APTE population — i.e., those on welfare who are considered employable. Knowing some of the characteristics of the employable unemployed of the Quebec welfare population will shed some light on who exactly is on welfare, what barriers they face in entering the work force and the general dynamics of poverty.

A Profile of the APTE Population

Who are the "employable unemployed?" Given that most Canadians believe welfare recipients should be working for their benefits,[15] it is worth analyzing some characteristics of the APTE population to know how feasible this is. The following gives a snapshot of the APTE adult population:

■ 52 percent of APTE recipients are women;

■ 40 percent are between the ages of 30 and 44, 33 percent between 18 and 29 and 27 percent are 45 or older (see figure 2);

■ About 60 percent are single, and about 25 percent are single parents (both proportions much higher than in the population as a whole; see figure 3);

■ 73 percent have not completed high school and 23 percent have 12 or more years of education;[16] and

■ 31 percent have been on welfare for less than 2 years; 36 percent have been on for six years or more (see figure 4).[17]

Thus, on the whole, half of the welfare population is employable, and a third are children. Of those employable, most are single, relatively young, with less than a high school education, and a third of them leave welfare within two years. In addition, single parents are highly represented.

Categorization Within APTE

In the APTE program, welfare recipients are divided into four categories, according to their ability to work and their willingness to participate

Figure 2

Distribution of Adults on APTE, According to Age, March 1993

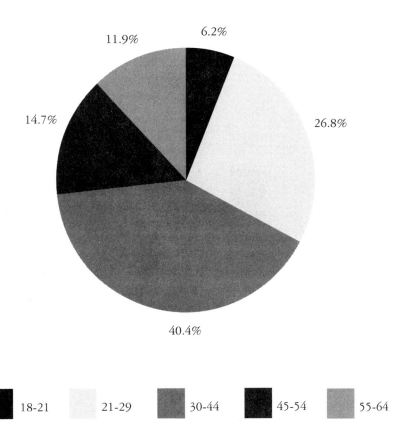

SOURCE: Ministère de la Sécurité du Revenu du Québec, "Rapport Statistique 1992-93".

Figure 3

Distribution of APTE Households and All Quebec Households by Household Type, March 1991

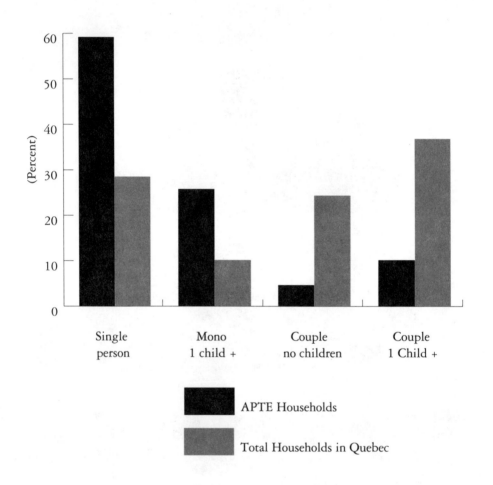

SOURCES: Ministère de la Sécurité du revenu du Québec, "Rapport Statistique 1991-92" and Statistics Canada, cat. 93-312, The Nation.

Figure 4

Distribution of Households on APTE According to the Number of Years on Welfare, March 1994

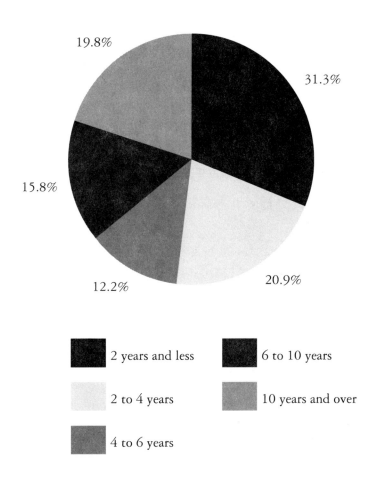

SOURCE: Ministère de la Sécurité du revenu, "Rapport statistique mensuel," mars 1994.

in welfare-to-work programs. No programs are mandatory, but benefits increase according to the level of interest in the employability programs. Thus, as we see in figure 5, single people on welfare who are "non-participants" would receive $6,281 per annum, $7,496 if they were unavailable and $10,729 if they were to earn the minimum wage. Total monthly benefits, including earnings exemptions, never exceed the monthly income from working at the minimum wage (for single individuals). The following are the four categories:

Unavailable (33.4 percent of the APTE total): Recipients may show an interest in programs, but their current situation prevents them from participating. This may be because they are: over 55 years of age; temporarily mentally or physically incapacitated; pregnant; in charge of dependent children (i.e., those six years of age or younger); or looking after someone who needs constant care.

Available (11.2 percent): Clients who are willing to participate in the employment enhancement programs, but for whom there are no spaces available.

Participant (11.3 percent): People who are enrolled in one of the welfare-to-work programs.

Non-participant (44.1 percent): People who do not want to participate in a program and who will look for a job on their own, or who have finished a program and have not indicated interest in another one.

Out of a total of 440,435 adults in APTE, only 49,846 are engaged in some form of government training, education or work program, while another 49,139 are waiting for places.

Some general comments can be made about the clientele in each group.[18] First, the unavailable category (147,314 people or one-third of the APTE total) could technically be regarded as part of the "unemployable" category of welfare. Those people classified as unavailable are primarily single mothers of young children; indeed, 42 percent of those unavailable cite caring for children (who are either under six years of age or handicapped) as the main reason for their unavailability. The second most cited reason for being unavailable is age: 35 percent of those unavailable are over 55 (mostly men), and are thus exempt from participating in programs.

Among the available population, 85 percent come from single households, while almost 60 percent have been on welfare for two years or less. Sixty percent are 30 or older.

Figure 5

Disposable Income[1] by Household for Minimum Wage Workers[2] and APTE Clients, March 1994

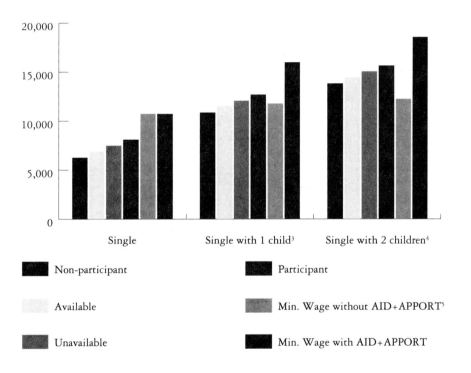

■ Non-participant	■ Participant
▨ Available	▨ Min. Wage without AID+APPORT[5]
▨ Unavailable	▨ Min. Wage with AID+APPORT

[1] Net taxes and transfers.
[2] Assumes 40-hour work at $5.85 per hour.
[3] Child care costs estimated at $2,150.
[4] Assumes child care costs of $3,120 for a child under age six and another under age 12.
[5] APPORT is an income supplement program which aids working-poor families. AID refers to special benefits to cover such things as medical costs, housing or transfortation costs.

SOURCE: Ministère de la Sécurité du revenu du Québec, Département des politiques et des programmes de la sécurité du revenu, mars 1994.

With regard to participants, 67 percent are from single households, and another 28 percent are from single-parent households. Forty percent of participant households have been on welfare for less than two years, and 27 percent for six years or more. Fifty-eight percent of participants are 30 years of age or older.

Finally, of the 194,136 non-participants, 74 percent are single adults. Almost a third of non-participants have been on welfare for less than two years, while 38 percent have been on welfare for six years or more. Seventy percent are over the age of 30.

Thus, there is a higher percentage of people who have been on welfare for two years or less and who can be expected to have a greater attachment to the labour force among the participant and available groups than among the non-participant and unavailable groups. Also, the participant and available categories have a higher percentage of their populations under age 30.

In summary, the actual percentage of the welfare population that is employable decreases from 56 percent to 37 percent if we exclude those considered "unavailable." Participants and those available to participate (approximately 100,000 people) represent 14 percent of the entire welfare population. Those not willing to participate in the government education and training programs, even though they receive lower benefits as a consequence, account for 23 percent of the welfare population.

THE PAIE PROGRAM

The Quebec PAIE program, introduced in May 1990, places welfare recipients with a public or private sector employer for six months. To be eligible, recipients must have been on welfare for at least six of the previous 12 months, and those who have been on for longer periods of time are favoured. Ideally, the employer has indicated his or her intent to hire someone permanently or for a season (at least 18 weeks), and the job must entail a minimum of 35 hours of work a week. Part-time jobs are also eligible, as long as the revenue is greater than the amount of welfare payments. Participants continue to receive the extended health care benefits (eye and dental care) they were entitled to as welfare recipients.

PAIE jobs are subsidized for a maximum of 26 weeks (six months). The employer is encouraged to hire the employee unless he or she has not performed adequately. Participants who fail to secure a job after the program can at this point qualify for Unemployment Insurance (UI). Because UI is a self-funded federal program, the Government of Quebec does not have to pay income security support to these former participants while they are on UI.

Concerns over potential abuse by employers who "churn" employees have been addressed by prohibiting those employers who fire participants without what is deemed to be just cause to participate in the program again for a specified amount of time. Also, before engaging a PAIE participant, the employer must inform the government of the number of employees in the department in which the PAIE employee will be working, and the hours worked per week over the previous six months. The employer must agree not to fire any other employees or reduce working hours to make room for the PAIE worker, and the government may verify this over time.

Table 2 outlines the subsidies to different types of employers. The subsidies are based on gross salary.

The maximum government subsidy for jobs in the public and non-profit sector is based on the minimum wage ($5.85 in March 1994). A single, non-participant welfare recipient would receive $3,000 over the same six month period ($500 per month gross). That results in a difference of $1,160 compared to the private sector PAIE subsidy and $2,324 compared to public and non-profit sector PAIE subsidy.

Approximately half of the PAIE participants work in the private sector, and the other half in the public and non-profit sector. Most of the employers participating in the program are small to medium-size businesses. Some of the larger, better known employers include such companies as Zellers, Canadian Tire, Pizza Hut, Plastibec, Metro, Harveys, Jean Coutu, La Baie, and Rotisserie Saint-Hubert.[19]

Between March 1990 and March 1993, 33,703 people participated in PAIE, with approximately 1,100 new participants every month during fiscal 1992-93. The Quebec government announced in November 1993 that it intended to create another 17,000 places for PAIE participants over the subsequent three years,[20] but revealed a mere 10 months later that only $10 million of a forecast budget of $72 million was left to pay for the program. Thus, enrolment of new participants was temporarily suspended.[21]

Profile of PAIE Participants

What do we know about those who participate in PAIE? First, they are primarily men (58 percent), and primarily unattached individuals

Table 2
PAIE Subsidies

Type of Employer	Subsidy (%)	Maximum Subsidy Per Week	Maximum Total Cost (26 weeks)
Private	66.6	$160	$4,160
Public	100	$204.75	$5,324
Non-Profit	100	$204.75	$5,324

SOURCE: Ministère de la Sécurité du Revenu

(67 percent). Sixteen percent of participants are single parents. The vast majority (85 percent) are under 45, and half of the total are between 30 and 44 years of age.

Is the program recruiting the most "job-ready" of the welfare population? Two statistics — related to education levels and the length of time on welfare — are revealing. PAIE participants are better educated (35 percent have 12 years or more of education) than either participants in all APTE employment-related programs (of whom 28 percent have 12 years or more) or the total social assistance population deemed to be employable and placed in the APTE category (of whom 23 percent have 12 years or more).

With regard to length of time on welfare, both PAIE participants and the larger group of participants in all APTE employment-related programs show similar experience: in both cases, 36 percent have been on welfare for less than two years, while approximately 30 percent have been on for six years or more. Of the total APTE population, 31 percent have been on welfare for under two years and 36 percent have been on for six years or more.

Thus, PAIE participants are, on average, slightly better educated and have been on welfare for a shorter time than the total number of employable unemployed. However, the differences are not great, and the profile of PAIE participants is on the whole similar to the total APTE population. Therefore, the basic characteristics of the PAIE group do not suggest they are significantly more job-ready than non-participants in PAIE. While other characteristics may suggest otherwise, they are not captured in this data.

Evaluation

In 1991, the Quebec government set out to evaluate the effectiveness of the six APTE employment development programs, including PAIE. Effectiveness, or success, is understood as integrating participants into the labour force and reducing their reliance on welfare. The methodology for all program evaluations consists of identifying two groups: participants and a comparison group that does not participate, both sharing similar characteristics (age, sex, education, years on welfare *etc.*). The comparison group is made up of those who either chose not to participate or who made themselves available but were not chosen due to lack of available spaces. Attachment to the labour market and reliance on welfare are monitored over a period of time. Between 1991 and 1993, people who were part of the APTE population over a specific period of time were interviewed by telephone. The interviews provided data on the employment history over the medium term (seven months) and long term (19 months) of welfare recipients who had and had not participated in the programs.

Each person's characteristics were weighted in order to standardize the sample. At seven months, 8,000 people were interviewed and of this number, 70 percent or 5,600 responded at 19 months. For the PAIE program, the weighted sample sizes consisted of 1,673 PAIE participants and 1,625 in the comparison group.

A potential for selection bias exists because some PAIE participants might be identified as "ready" or "almost ready" for employment. However, the numbers of such participants is small (estimated at 5 percent) and not considered significant by the evaluators of the program.[22] Another possible source of selection bias is the fact that the comparison group consists of individuals who either chose not to participate in employment-related programs or made themselves available, but were told that there was no room in any suitable program. Thus, the comparison group may be systematically different from the PAIE participants in terms of employment potential, despite their similarities in terms of observable characteristics such as age, sex, education and time spent on welfare. These potential biases should be kept in mind when reviewing the results.

Rate of Integration into the Labour Force

PAIE had the highest success rate among the six employment enhancement programs in integrating participants into the work force. (See appendix for a description of all of the programs, as well as a figure summarizing the results.) This is not surprising given that PAIE employers are chosen based on the likelihood that they will hire participants following the subsidized employment period.

Seventy percent of PAIE participants had at least one job over the 19 months following their training and work experience, compared to 33 percent of the comparison group (see figure 6). Seventy-four percent whose PAIE experience was in the private sector had at least one job; the corresponding figure for those with PAIE experience in the public and non-profit sector was 65 percent.

Figure 6

Percentage Employed At Least Once Over 19 Months and At 19 Months

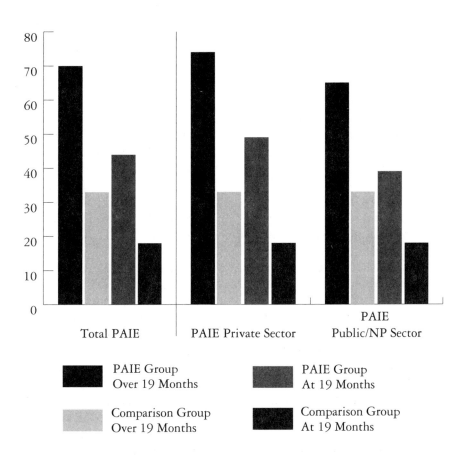

SOURCE: Ministère de la Sécurité du revenu du Québec, "Relance auprès des prestataires de la sécurité du revenu ayant participé à un programme de développement de l'employabilité ou d'intégration en emploi: Deuxième volet" ("Relance deux"), février 1994.

However, only 44 percent of PAIE participants were employed at the time of the interview 19 months after their PAIE experience, compared to 18 percent of the comparison group. Again, there was approximately a 10 percentage point difference between those whose PAIE experience was in the private sector (49 percent employed after 19 months) *versus* the public sector (39 percent). Perhaps the most telling number regarding the rate of integration into the labour force is found in figure 7. Of those PAIE participants employed at least once over the 19 months, 30 percent worked the entire period. Of comparison group members employed at least once, just seven percent worked the entire 19 months.

Two further comparisons provide more details about employment prospects after participation in PAIE. First, once participants found a job, 55 percent worked continuously from that point until the end of the study (58 percent for those whose PAIE experience was in the private sector and 50 percent for those whose PAIE experience was in the public and non-profit sector). Once comparison group members found a job, 48 percent worked continuously until the end of the study. This suggests that, while PAIE, on the whole, leads to the integration of more people into the labour force, it has less of an effect on the permanent rate of employment once people find a job, particularly in the case of those whose experience was in the public and non-profit sector.

However, of the PAIE participants who found a job, 63 percent left welfare for the remainder of the 19-month evaluation period, compared to 49 percent of those in the comparison group who found jobs (see figure 8). PAIE participants in the private sector had a higher exit rate by 15 percentage points than PAIE participants in the public and non-profit sector (69 percent *versus* 54 percent). Of course, we do not know just how permanent this effect is, since it only covers a 19-month period.

Thus, regarding the rate of integration into the labour force, we can conclude that the PAIE program is most effective in helping people find jobs, given the much higher rates of employment in general and the solid 30 percent of participants who were employed for the full 19 months. On the other hand, once people find a job, there is little difference between the PAIE and comparison groups regarding whether they kept that job continuously over the period of the study. However, welfare costs were reduced: a higher proportion of PAIE participants than comparison group members stayed off welfare after finding a job.

Figure 7

Percentage Employed For The Full 19 Months Among Those Employed At Least Once

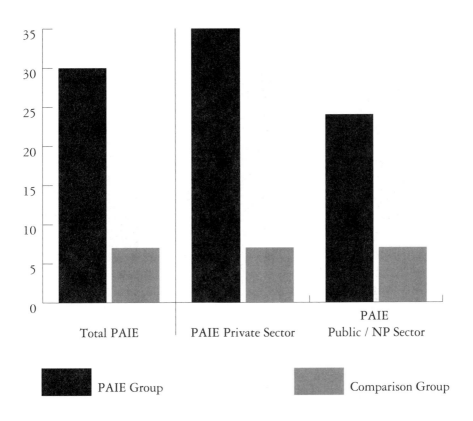

Figure 8

Exit Rate From Welfare:
Percentage of Those Employed At Least Once
Who Did Not Return To Welfare

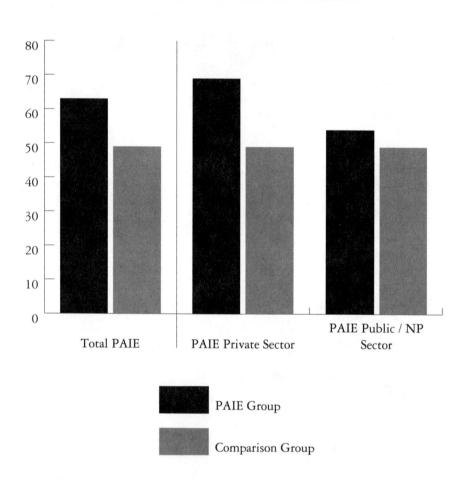

SOURCE: Ministère de la Sécurité du revenu du Québec, "Relance deux," février 1994.

Employment After PAIE

Below, we look at the kinds of jobs PAIE participants found after participating in the program.

First, and perhaps most importantly when assessing the success of PAIE, we must look at the number of subsidized jobs found after participating in PAIE. Once a participant completes the PAIE program and finds a job, he or she may still end up in a job subsidized by the provincial or federal government under a separate employment and training program.

Of those who worked at least once following their PAIE experience, 17 percent had a subsidized job as their first work experience and 29 percent were employed *at least once* in a subsidized job, compared to eight percent and 10 percent respectively of comparison group members who found jobs. This suggests that, whatever the gains in employment integration, the PAIE results must be discounted to reflect continued government subsidies through employment.

Jobs: Where? How Much? How Long?

Approximately 75 percent of both the PAIE and comparison groups found their jobs in the service sector. This is not surprising, as Quebec has seen the greatest employment growth in this sector over the past five years, with a net increase in jobs of 91,000 over 1988-93 compared to a net loss of 112,000 in other sectors.[23]

In the PAIE group, most jobs were found in personnel administration (27 percent), specialty services (18 percent) and manufacturing (15 percent). The comparison group showed similar results, although significantly fewer jobs were found in personnel (9 percent).

For both the PAIE and comparison groups, more than 70 percent of the jobs found were in the private sector. Sixty-nine percent of the jobs held by PAIE participants were permanent, compared to 51 percent for the comparison group. PAIE participants worked 35 hours per week on average, compared to 32.7 hours for the comparison group.

Of PAIE participants who found a job, almost half did so within one month of leaving PAIE. This is not surprising given that many PAIE participants go on to work for their current employer. Twenty-nine percent found a job within two to six months. Of comparison group members who found a job, only 16 percent did so within one month, but 53 percent found one within two to six months.

How long did they have these jobs? Table 3 shows the breakdown of consecutive months employed. On average, 39 percent of PAIE participants were employed for more than a year (13 to 18 months) with the highest rate for those whose PAIE experience was in the private sector (46 percent). For the comparison group, 32 percent worked for the same period of time. Close to half of the comparison group worked only one to six months consecutively (compared to 35 percent for the PAIE group), which may reflect the higher number of temporary jobs. For both groups, over 60 percent of those employed are in work for a year or less. The extent to which these numbers are driven by the volatile labour market or the attractions of UI is unclear. But if the most employable of the welfare population are finding work for only a year on average, then the impression of a cyclical dynamic of poverty and welfare use is quite accurate.

Table 4 shows gross hourly wages broken down by type of job. The comparison group earned on average a dollar more than the PAIE group ($9.35 *versus* $8.30). Therefore, participating in PAIE does not result in higher wages.

On a final note regarding employment, when asked how they found their job, 30 percent of the PAIE group said through an employment program, 25 percent through a friend or acquaintance, 15 percent by going directly to the employer and another 15 percent through an employment centre. In contrast, almost none of the comparison group found jobs through programs. Forty-two percent found them through an acquaintance and 21 percent by going directly to employers. Another 12 percent found them through newspaper want ads.

When asked whether they were satisfied with the job they had found, over 80 percent of the PAIE and comparison groups said yes. Given that respondents had been unemployed for more than six months, one could expect such a response. In any case, it appears that PAIE does no better in matching workers with satisfactory jobs than non-participants do themselves.

Substitution Effects

Much has been written about the displacement effects created by subsidized employment programs, and other similar employment enhancement programs.[24] Broadly speaking, there are two major types of displacement effects that are of concern in the context of a program such as PAIE. First, deadweight displacement occurs when a subsidy is given

Table 3

Consecutive Months Employed:
PAIE Participants and Comparison Group

	1-6 Months	7-12 Months	13-18 Months
PAIE Participants	35%	26%	39%
PAIE Private Sector	40%	24%	46%
PAIE Public / NP Sector	41%	28%	31%
Comparison Group	49%	19%	32%

SOURCE: Ministère de la Sécurité du revenu du Québec, "Relance deux," février 1994.

Table 4

Gross Hourly Wage ($) of PAIE Participants and Comparison Group

			Type of Job			
	Average Salary	Median Salary	Permanent	Temporary	Subsidized	Non-Subsidized
PAIE Participants	8.30	7.67	8.05	8.63	8.06	8.45
Comparison Group	9.35	-	8.96	9.46	8.18	9.50

SOURCE: Ministère de la Sécurité du revenu du Québec, "Relance deux," février 1994.

to a worker who would have found a job anyway, or to an employer who would have hired someone even without the subsidy. Concerns over selection bias and creaming in employment enhancement programs are directly related to this type of displacement. Second, substitution effects occur when employers hire subsidized workers, thereby substituting them for unsubsidized workers (this effect can also fall into the larger category of deadweight displacement). In the worst case scenario, employers let go of someone else to make room for the subsidized worker.

A number of statistical, analytical and theoretical methods have been created to allow us to measure displacement effects, though no method is considered fully accurate. Estimates of the substitution effects of certain job creation programs range from 20 percent to 70 percent (i.e., 20 to 70 percent of the net job creation is attributable to substitution effects).[25]

Given the difficulty in measuring such effects, the task becomes one of designing such programs so as to maximize their effect on the target group. In defence of such programs, it is argued that an unsubsidized worker who is displaced will have a much greater chance of finding employment than the subsidized, hard-to-employ worker. Broader objectives of equality of opportunity and income redistribution may be served.

The PAIE program, by its very design, creates displacement effects in the private sector. Employers are sought who are in general intending to hire someone. In a poll of PAIE employers taken in March 1991, 1,600 employers were asked what they would have done if the PAIE program did not exist and they did not have a subsidized employee. Employers in the private and public/non-profit sectors were asked to choose among four responses:

1. The work done by the subsidized employee would have been divided among the other workers.
2. Someone would have been hired to do the work.
3. None of the work would have been done.
4. The work would have been divided among non-salaried workers.

Their responses are broken down below:

	Private Sector (%)	Public/Non-profit Sector (%)
Response 1	37.6	28.8
Response 2	51.6	10.0
Response 3	9.2	27.4
Response 4	0.8	27.3

Granting that the methodology may be imperfect, the most reveal-ing statistic among the above is found in response number two, which suggests a 50 percent substitution effect in the private sector. The public sector shows little effect: understandably, given the consistent shortage of funds there.

The substitution effect is significant, and suggests that program co-ordinators must be rigorous in targeting the most vulnerable unem-ployed. The primary aim of the program is to get welfare recipients, who have been on welfare for at least six months, back into the labour force, to prevent some of the negative effects of long-term unemployment. As we saw from previous statistics, the PAIE program seems to do a fairly good job of this given that more than 60 percent of participants have been on welfare for two years or more.

Cost-Benefit Analysis

In the absence of an extensive cost-benefit analysis of the PAIE pro-gram (the Government of Quebec is expected to release one later this year), we are left with a back-of-the-envelope analysis of the cost effec-tiveness of the program. There are a multitude of variables to consider when attempting this, not to mention the effects of the cost-sharing sys-tem between the provinces and Ottawa. Therefore, what follows can only be a rough estimate of the basic costs and benefits of the program.

It was noted earlier that a PAIE subsidy represents between $4,160 and $5,324 (over six months). In comparison, a single person on welfare for six months would receive $3,000 ($500 per month). Thus, the PAIE subsidy costs an extra $1,160 to $2,324, before overhead costs. Let us assume that the average extra cost is $1,700 and average overhead costs are $850 (50 percent of subsidy).[26] This suggests that the total cost of the PAIE subsidy (above equivalent welfare costs) is $2,550. In addition, we assume all participants are single individuals. (Single parents receive a higher amount of welfare. Thus, we err on the conservative side.)

In the 19 months following the end of their PAIE experience, partic-ipants worked an average of 7.6 months. Comparison group members worked for only 2.8 months on average.[27] If the comparison group expe-rience reflects what would have happened to PAIE participants in the absence of PAIE, one can say that PAIE generates 4.8 extra months of work for the average participant. This also represents 4.8 months that the participant is not on welfare. The Government of Quebec thus saves

$2,400 in welfare costs (4.8 months x $500/month) per participant. Therefore, the net cost per PAIE participant is $150, $2,400 in welfare savings offset by the $2,550 cost of the PAIE subsidy.

From the perspective of the Government of Quebec, there could be additional fiscal savings, as those who do not find a job can go on to UI. And, of course, the welfare savings estimated above are based only on the first 19 months following the PAIE experience and could continue to grow over time.

Of course the list of what this calculation does not take into account is substantial: medical and child care benefits, the number of subsidized jobs (a quarter of the total), substitution effects (roughly estimated at one half in the private sector, as discussed above; however, one cannot assume that those substituted automatically become dependent on income security programs), and the time value of money (a dollar of PAIE subsidy today is worth more than a dollar of welfare saving later). Therefore, it would be premature to state on the basis of this calculation that this program is cost-effective.

Summary

In summary, the PAIE program is successful at integrating participants into the labour force. Compared to a comparison group of other welfare beneficiaries, PAIE participants experienced more attachment to the work force, and a smaller but significant number were employed over the entire 19 months of the study. Participants also left welfare at a higher rate. Participants worked more hours over a slightly longer period of time, but did not receive higher wages.

The program does an adequate job of targeting the long-term unemployed: the majority of participants (63 percent) have been on welfare for over two years. Regarding cost, it is too early to say that the program is cost-effective.

Evaluations from the US

A brief mention should be made of the subsidized employment programs that have been conducted in the US since the 1970s. The evaluations of these programs represent the best information we have on a relatively long-term basis for such programs. Four different types of projects were conducted between the 1970s and late 1980s that varied

greatly in design, the demographics of the project site and target populations.[28] All four experiments are considered selective-voluntary demonstrations, which means that participants volunteered and, in some cases,
were screened to meet certain criteria. The demonstrations were of two
types: a small-scale evaluation that tests a specific program; and a larger-
scale multi-state program.

While these programs differ in many ways, they were all based on a
similar formula aimed at reintroducing welfare recipients into the labour
force. Participants, for the most part single-parent mothers, were provided a number of weeks of training and then a subsidized job either in the
private or public sector.

The following general conclusions can be made:

- Participation in a program had a positive impact on earnings
  over an extended period of time; earnings increased in the range
  of $590 to $4,800 three years after participation[29];
- Welfare dependence declined though by a lesser amount; welfare
  savings ranged from a net cost of $80 to savings of $400[30];
- Such programs can be cost-effective from the government's perspective, though results are varied;
- While earnings increased, they did not increase by substantial
  amounts. Peoples' standards of living may have changed but
  theses changes did not lift people out of poverty.

One can debate whether studies conducted in the US have comparative value for Canadian research. Unlike in Canada, the US welfare population is overwhelmingly single-parent mothers (90%) with a larger
percentage of visible minorities. As in many provinces in Canada, however, some studies suggest three quarters of the welfare population are
able to work.[31]

The impact of these programs is not monumental, but neither is it
insignificant. If one believes that the government has a role to play on the
supply-side of the employment equation, then one can conclude that a well-
designed, well-targeted program may constitute a good use of public funds.

CONCLUSION

The evidence from this chapter suggests that subsidized employment programs have a positive impact on integrating welfare recipients
into the labour force. It should be remembered that the success of these

programs may be overshadowed by the importance of such macroeconomic factors as the regional employment rate. All the same, carefully constructed programs may be an efficient use of public funds for several reasons. First and foremost, such programs help reintegrate many long-term unemployed into "legitimate" jobs — i.e., not just make-work jobs. Second, subsidized employment programs embody the new orientation of welfare policy. Such programs not only end the passive cash transfer system that has been the norm in income security programs in general, but also emphasize the integration of social and labour market policies. Given the new realities of the labour market, such an integration is critical to combatting economic insecurity in society. Third, they reassure taxpayers that the system is not being abused and that welfare recipients are not getting a "free ride."

In the end, the most critical factor in the success of programs may be the level of public funding. As the PAIE example in Quebec illustrates, budget constraints can hinder the most promising of policies.[32]

1. "No Free Lunch for the Jobless," *The Economist*, August 20, 1994, p. 55.

2. See The Family Support Act of 1988, US Congress as well as the Four Corners Agreement of 1985, ministries of Health and Welfare Canada and Employment and Immigration Canada.

3. See Judith Gueron and Edward Pauly, *Welfare to Work* (New York: Russell Sage Foundation, 1990), p. 4. For an in-depth review of evaluation methodology, see Charles Manski and Irwin Garfinkel, *Evaluation of Employment and Training Programs* (Cambridge, Mass.: Harvard University Press). Difficulties in Canadian data are explained in Surendra Gera, *Creating Jobs in the Private Sector: Evidence from the Canadian Employment Tax Credit Program* (Ottawa: Economic Council of Canada and Minister of Supply and Services, 1988), p. 49.

4. The Four Corners Agreement of 1985 is called such because it was signed by the federal ministries of Health and Welfare and Employment and Immigration and their provincial counterparts.

5. Statistics Canada, *Provincial Economic Accounts*, Cat. 13-213; 1986 dollars.

6. See Paul A.R. Hobson and France St-Hilaire, *Toward Sustainable Federalism: Reforming Federal-Provincial Fiscal Arrangements* (Montreal: Institute for Research on Public Policy, 1993), p. 54.

7. See James Iain Gow, Alain Noël and Patrick Villeneuve, "Choc des valeurs dans l'aide sociale au Québec? Pertinence et signification des visites à domicile," Cahiers du GRETSE, No. 13, Université de Montréal.

8. See National Council of Welfare, *Welfare Incomes 1993* (Ottawa: Minister of Supply and Services Canada, 1994), p. 35.

9. See Surendra Gera, David Caldwell and David Ferguson, "Industrial Restructuring in Canadian Manufacturing: A Comparison Between the Early 1980s and 1990s," paper presented at the Canadian Employment Research Forum Conference, Ottawa, March 5, 1993.

10. Canadian Press, "Chômage: le taux naturel situé entre 6 et 8%," *La Presse*, June 10, 1994, p. 2.

11. See Gera, Caldwell and Ferguson, "Industrial Restructuring."

12. See Monique Tremblay, "Evaluation des expériences acquises par les prestataires participants aux programmes PAIE, PSMT et EXTRA: Le point de vue des employeurs," Ministère de la Main-d'oeuvre, de la Sécurité du revenu et de la Formation professionnelle (Québec, 1992).

13. See H.M. Brenner, *Mental Illness and the Economy* (Cambridge: Cambridge University Press, 1984); and P. Kelvin and J.E. Jarrett, *Unemployment - Its Social and Psychological Effects* (Cambridge: Cambridge University Press, 1984).

14. All yearly statistics used in this chapter are based on March 1994 data unless specified otherwise.

15. Gallup Poll, March 31, 1994, Gallup Canada.

16. These figures confirm recent work suggesting that the private rate of return (i.e., to the individual) resulting from finishing high school is 20 percent for men and 35 percent for women. See François Vaillancourt, "Private and Public Monetary Returns to Schooling in Canada, 1985," Working Paper No. 35, (Ottawa: Economic Council of Canada, 1992), p. 20.

17. See the Economic Council of Canada, *The New Face of Poverty: Income Security Needs of Canadian Families* (Ottawa: Ministry of Supply and Services Canada, 1992), p. 22.

18. The following statistics regarding the characteristics of each category are based on the March 1993 figures.

19. Information provided by staff of the Direction des politiques et des programmes du développement de l'employabilité of the Ministère de la Main-d'oeuvre, de la Sécurité du revenu et de la Formation professionnelle du Québec.

20. *La Presse*, May 27, 1994, p. A2.

21. "Faute de fonds, Québec ralentit un programme 'qui marche bien'," *La Presse*, September 8, 1994, p. A1.

22. Conversation with Director of Research, Evaluation and Statistics, Quebec Ministry of Manpower, Income Security and Training, April 1994.

23. Figures from Statistics Canada, Survey of the Active Population, calculated by the Policy and Liaison Federal Office of Regional Development of Quebec.

24. For a review of much of the literature, see Paul Dickinson, *The Displacement Effect of Employment Enhancement Programs and Wage*

Subsidies, Social Policy Division, Policy, Planning and Information Branch, Health and Welfare, Fall 1990. See also, Monique Tremblay, *Evaluation des expériences acquises par les prestataires participants aux programmes PAIE, PSMT et EXTRA: Le point de vue des employeurs*, Ministère de la Main-d'oeuvre, de la Sécurité du revenu et de la Formation professionnelle, (Québec, Avril, 1992), and John L. Palmer (ed.), *Creating Jobs: Public Employment Programs and Wage Subsidies*, (Washington: The Brookings Institution, 1978).

25. See Tremblay, *Evaluation des expériences*, p. 103.

26. The figure of 50 percent for overhead costs was suggested as a fair assumption by US experts consulted by the author.

27. The average number of months worked for PAIE participants and comparison group members is based on information on the work experiences of the groups contained in figure 7 and table 3.

28. The four programs are The National Supported Work Demonstration, The New Jersey and Maine On-The-Job Training programs, the AFDC Homemaker-Home Health Aide Demonstration and the National JTPA Study. For an overview of all the projects see Gueron and Pauly, *Welfare to Work*, particularly pp. 172 and 173, 192-215; and Robert J. Lalonde, "The Earnings Impact of US Employment and Training Programs," University of Chicago, paper presented at the Conference on Policy Research in Training, Unemployment, Income Support and Immigration, revised, December 1992. For details on the National Supported Work Demonstration, see Kenneth Couch, "New Evidence on the Long-Term Effects of Employment Training Programs," *Journal of Labour Economics*, Vol. 10, no. 4 (1992), p. 385. For details of the AFDC-Homemaker project see Stephen Bell and Larry L. Orr, "Is Subsidized Employment Cost Effective for Welfare Recipients?", *The Journal of Human Resources*, Vol. 29, no. 1 (Winter 1994). For a detailed analysis of the JTPA Study, see Howard S. Bloom, Larry Orr *et al.*, "The National JTPA Study Overview: Impacts, Benefits, and Costs of Title II-A," Abt Associates, January and March 1994.

29. The figure $590 is two years after participation in the New Jersey Program (see Gueron and Pauly, *Welfare to Work*, p. 173); the figure $4,800 is 30 months after participation in the JTPA study (see

Bloom, Orr, *et al.*, "JTPA Study Overview", March 1994, p. 139).

30. Figures from Gueron and Pauly, *Welfare to Work*, p. 173. Figures for JTPA study are not available.

31. Nicholas Zill, "Potential Exemptions," presentation at the American Enterprise Institute for Public Policy Research, Linking Welfare to Work Conference, December 15, 1993, Washington, pp. 3-10.

32. I would like to thank IRPP President Monique Jérôme-Forget for giving me the opportunity to work on these issues and for her guidance and support during the research and writing of this chapter. I would also like to thank my IRPP colleagues France St-Hilaire, Adil Sayeed, François Vaillancourt and especially Michel Leblanc for their excellent comments on earlier drafts. Cyril Battini and particularly Stéphane Fortin were extremely generous with their time in helping put together the graphs and tables. Chantal Létourneau was expert as always at solving word-processing glitches. And finally Mathew Horsman provided excellent suggestions of a copy-editing nature as well as general good cheer.

RS — Rattrapage scolaire (Remedial Education)

This program offers basic or vocational education to help participants obtain a high school degree. Courses are offered in specific skill areas, reading and writing and French for non-francophones. Participants must have been out of school full time for at least the preceding nine months. Priority is given to people who left their studies more than two years before applying.

Participants must be in class for at least 60 hours a month and prepare a plan of action for return to the labour force after their course. Participants receive special benefits of $500 a year for education costs and $10 a day for child care.

REPS — Retour aux études postsecondaires pour les chefs de famille monoparentale (Return to Post-secondary Studies for Single Parents)

Offered only to single parents, REPS provides post-secondary education (college ["CÉGEP"] or university). Participants must have been on welfare for a total of 24 months out of the preceding 36 months and be studying full time. Participants can be enrolled for a maximum of four sessions within a period of 24 months.

Special benefits are given to participants, including $10 a day for child care, coverage of educational costs and a maximum of $200 for travel.

EXTRA — Expérience de travail (Community Service Work)

EXTRA provides 20 hours of work per week in non-profit and charity organizations. The program is targeted at people who are considered to face some barriers to integrating into the labour market. Clients must have been on welfare for at least a year, and participate in EXTRA for at most a year. The work is meant to familiarize individuals with the working environment and improve work habits. Examples of jobs include serving food at schools or cleaning for non-profit organizations.

SEMO — Services externes de main-d'oeuvre (External Labour Services)

SEMO is targeted to individuals who have mental or physical problems, such as the handicapped, alcoholics, juvenile delinquents or those who have received psychiatric treatment. SEMO participants work in non-profit organizations for a minimum of 20 hours a week and are paid the minimum wage for a maximum of six weeks. They are also given $10 a day for child care.

SMT — Stage en milieu de travail (Apprenticeship Program)

SMT offers short-term or long-term apprenticeships and is available to adults who have finished or quit school at least six months before. Private businesses create a post in which the apprentice will fulfil identified tasks and receive training transferable to other jobs. The business must also assign a tutor to the apprentice to oversee his or her training and performance. Long-term apprenticeships cover a period of between 13 and 52 weeks; short-term apprenticeships range from four to 12 weeks. Apprentices must work at least 20 hours a week.

The employer is required to pay the apprentice a minimum of $100 a month. The government will subsidize the employer an average amount of $400 per month.

Appendix Figure
Percentage Employed At Least Once Over 19 Months and At 19 Months

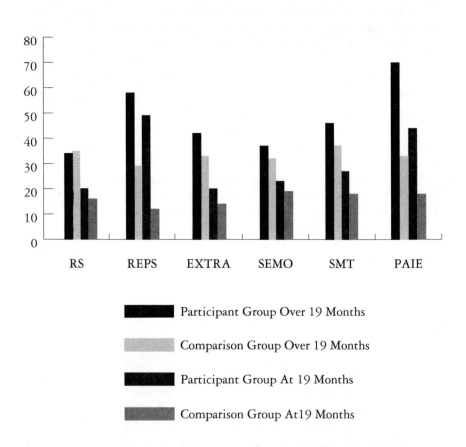

SOURCE: Ministère de la Sécurité du revenu du Québec, "Relance deux," février 1994.

Patricia M. Evans is an Associate Professor in the School of Social Work at York University in Toronto. Her areas of research include women and social policy and comparative income security, with particular reference to single mothers. She is co-editor of *Women's Caring: Feminist Perspectives on Social Welfare* (Toronto: McClelland & Stewart, 1991), and has contributed to journals in Canada and abroad.

Lesley A. Jacobs is Assistant Professor of Philosophy and of Law and Society at York University in Toronto. He completed his Ph.D. at Oxford University in England. His areas of research are social justice and American and Canadian social policy. He is the author of *Rights and Deprivation* (Oxford: Oxford University Press, 1993) and *The Democratic Vision of Politics* (Englewood Cliffs: Prentice-Hall, forthcoming) and the co-editor of *Out of Apathy* (London and New York: Verso, 1989).

Alain Noël is Assistant Professor of Political Science at the Université de Montréal. He completed his Ph.D. at the Graduate School of International Studies of the University of Denver and previously taught in the Department of Political Science of the University of Alberta. He has published articles in several academic journals as well as chapters in various books. He is co-editor of *L'espace québécois* (Montréal: Boréal, forthcoming) and of *Perspectivas sobre Quebec contemporánea* (Mexico: ITAM University Press, forthcoming) and associate editor of *Canadian Public Policy*.

Elisabeth B. Reynolds is a student in the economics program at Université de Montréal. Previously, she was a Policy Analyst at IRPP and co-ordinator of the Social Policy Program. She has also worked in the financial services sector and was the Charles H. Fiske Harvard Scholar at Trinity College, Cambridge.

SOCIAL POLICY:

Ross Finnie, *Child Support: The Guideline Options*

Elisabeth B. Reynolds (ed.), *Income Security: Changing Needs, Changing Means*

Jean-Michel Cousineau, *La Pauvreté et l'État: Pour un nouveau partage des compétences en matière de sécurité sociale*

CITY-REGIONS:

Andrew Sancton, *Governing Canada's City-Regions: Adapting Form to Function*

William Coffey, *The Evolution of Canada's Metropolitan Economies*

EDUCATION:

Bruce Wilkinson, *Educational Choice: Necessary But Not Sufficient*

Peter Coleman, *Learning About Schools: What Parents Need to Know and How They Can Find Out*

Edwin G. West, *Ending the Squeeze on Universities*

GOVERNANCE:

G. Bruce Doern, *The Road to Better Public Services: Progress Constraints in Five Canadian Federal Agencies*

Donald G. Lenihan, Gordon Robertson, Roger Tassé, *Canada: Reclaiming the Middle Ground*

F. Leslie Seidle (ed.), *Seeking a New Canadian Partnership: Asymmetrical and Confederal Options*

F. Leslie Seidle (ed.), *Equity and Community: The Charter, Interest Advocacy and Representation*

F. Leslie Seidle (ed.), *Rethinking Government: Reform or Reinvention?*

PUBLIC FINANCE:

Paul A.R. Hobson and France St-Hilaire, *Toward Sustainable Federalism: Reforming Federal-Provincial Fiscal Arrangements*

TELECOMMUNICATIONS:
Charles Sirois, Claude E. Forget, *The Medium and the Muse: Culture, Telecommunications and the Information Highway*
Charles Sirois, Claude E. Forget, *Le Médium et les Muses : la culture, les télécommunications et l'autoroute de l'information*

Choices\Choix —

SOCIAL SECURITY REFORM:
IRPP prend position / The IRPP Position
Commentaries on the Axworthy Green Paper

PUBLIC FINANCE:
Répartition régionale des dépenses fiscales touchant les corporations
À qui profitent les avantages fiscaux

HEALTH:
Les marchés internes dans le contexte canadien

These and other publications are available from:
Renouf Publishing
1294 Algoma Road
Ottawa, Ontario
K1B 3W8
Tel.: (613) 741-4333
Fax.: (613) 741-5439